MW01274310

How to Compete
in the WAR FOR
TALENT
A GUIDE TO HIRING THE BEST

Other Books of Interest:

DC Press

Raising Children One Day at a Time:
A Daily Survival Guide
for Committed Parents

Who's Right (Whose Right?):
Seeking Answers and Dignity in the
Debate Over the Right to Die

E-R: From Prevention to Triage
— How to Retain Key Employees

If It Weren't for You, We Could Get Along:
Stop Blaming and Start Living

InSync Press

Go for the Green!
Leadership Secrets from the Golf Course (the Front Nine)

366 Surefire Ways to Let Your Employees Know
They Count

Retain or Retrain:
How to Keep the Good Ones from Leaving

How to Compete
in WAR FOR
the TALENT
A GUIDE TO HIRING THE BEST

Carol A. Hacker

PRESS

A Division of the Diogenes Consortium

SANFORD • FLORIDA

Copyright © 2001 by Carol A. Hacker

All rights reserved. No part of this publication may be reproduced, stored in a retrieval system, or transmitted in any form or by any means — electronic, mechanical, photocopy, recording, or any other — except for brief quotations in printed reviews, without the prior permission of the publisher.

Published by DC Press
2445 River Tree Circle
Sanford, FL 32771
http://www.focusonethics.com
407-688-1156

This book was set in Trump Medieaval
Cover Design and Composition by Jonathan Pennell

Library of Congress Catalog Number: 2001087014
        Hacker, Carol A.
How to Compete in the War for Talent, A Guide to Hiring the Best
        ISBN: 0-9708444-4-1

First DC Press Edition
10   9   8   7   6   5   4   3   2   1
Printed in the United States of America

DISCLAIMER

THIS PUBLICATION is designed to provide accurate and authoritative information with regard to the subject matter covered. It is sold with the understanding that the publisher and the author are not engaged in rendering legal, accounting, or other professional services. If legal advice or other expert assistance is required, the services of a qualified professional person should be sought. (From a Declaration of Principles jointly adopted by a Committee of the American Bar Association and a Committee of Publishers and Associations).

DEDICATION

To the memory of my loving mother Virginia

ACKNOWLEDGEMENTS

MANY PEOPLE HAVE CONTRIBUTED to the success of this endeavor, especially Captain Peter Van Ness, USNR. You are truly the encouragement behind this book. Your military expertise, writing talent, and ability to help me stay focused chapter by chapter helped to make this project a success. The words "thank you" will never be enough.

Thank you Colonel Len Marrella, U.S. Army (Ret.) for your valuable insight.

Judy Rogers, you're a wonderful editor, writer and friend. Bill and Cher Holton, you are two of the most creative people I know. You've always been an inspiration to me.

Dennis McClellan, you're in a class by yourself! Thank you for believing in me once again. Thank you Marnee McClellan for your input on the cover. Your idea about the map was exactly what it needed.

Thank you Jonathan Pennell for a superb cover design and page layout. You are incredibly talented!

CONTENTS

ABOUT THE AUTHOR

CAROL HACKER is a high energy, value-added speaker, trainer and author. She has over two decades of human resource management experience and has been the president of Hacker & Associates since January 1989. Carol specializes in teaching executives, managers, supervisors, team leaders and business owners how to more effectively select and recruit top talent.

Carol has developed and implemented training programs for over 25,000 people in business, industry, and government. Her customized workshops, presented in a powerful, professional environment, have helped organizations of all sizes educate and motivate their leaders. She's worked with hundreds of corporations and associations including IBM Corporation, The Coca Cola Company, GE, Holiday Inn WorldWide, U.S. Postal Service, U.S. Department of the Treasury, Glaxo Wellcome, International Home Furnishings Association, Röder GmbH Germany, National Data Corporation, Sebastian International, Federal Reserve Bank,

Broadcast Cable Financial Management Association, BellSouth Information Systems, Emory University School of Medicine, National Hospice Organization and many more.

She's the author of over 100 published articles and 9 business books including the bestseller, *Hiring Top Performers-350 Great Interview Questions For People Who Need People.* Carol is a University of Wisconsin honors graduate where she earned her B.S. and M.S.

Carol's workshops are customized to meet your specific needs and include:

- How to Hire Top Performers

- How to Take the Guesswork Out of Interviewing

- Keeping Winners

- How to Build a Retention Culture

- 21st Century Strategies for Gaining Employee Loyalty and Reducing Turnover

- Coaching and Counseling Skills for Managers and Supervisors

- The Challenge of Leadership

- How to Conduct "Win-Win" Performance Appraisals

PUBLISHER'S COMMENT

FOR BUSINESSES—regardless of size—perhaps the most critical aspect of the operation is the roster of employees who staff the organization. Everyone knows that it is nearly impossible to get rid of certain bad employees; they seem to linger on like some winter virus that can't be shaken. And at the same time, it is often extremely difficult to keep good people from jumping ship and going where they think the grass is greener.

The search for, and hiring of, that "right person" is crucial. When you factor in the costs of rehiring and retraining, you can appreciate the negative financial impact such events can have on the company's bottom line. As in a military campaign, new-hire planning is undeniably essential to the eventual success of the process. Sometimes unlimited financial support isn't the answer. As many military powers have discovered, it's not the money available that wins battles, but the execution of well-established, well thought out campaigns that make winners out of even the supposed weaker or smaller of adversaries.

Carol Hacker has taken her more than two decades of experience and brought her own talents to the pages of this clearly conceived guide. There are many books available that offer recommendations on how to interview and hire prospective employees. Some focus on how to involve current staff in the hiring process, others on how to identify the incentives a company can wave in front of attractive recruits, and yet others address what to ask, how to ask and what the applicants' responses mean. Any combination of these will give you valuable information that you can use in your effort to create the ideal hiring scenario. In *How to Compete in the War for Talent*, the author has brought to bear best-practice ideas and validated experiences; she's molded them into one succinct book.

Let the message of this book meld with your company's philosophy. Keep in mind that even the most experienced and successful organizations can benefit from fine-tuning their approach to the hiring process.

The responsibility of finding and hiring the best people can be compared to warfare. Only those who are prepared— those who have thought through their company's mission and direction and who *understand* how and where new-hires fit into that structure will be victorious. Many will continue to lose small battles as well as the larger wars. Great products and great services are nothing without the best-qualified people in place to make them work.

Dennis McClellan
Publisher

INTRODUCTION

I CHOSE THE TITLE *How to Compete in the War for Talent* for this book because of the correlation between war and the challenges businesses face today in fighting for good people. It's hard to win a war without sufficient numbers of competent soldiers, sailors, marines and airmen. Nor can nations "effectively posture" with their adversaries without a firm base of solid, well-trained troops. And so it is in business.

War isn't usually rational. It can't always be won by applying time-honored principles and familiar practices. A current war shouldn't be fought using the last war's order of battle. However, there are a number of strategies for engaging in military conflict that can be applied to all manner of business from the boardroom, to manufacturing operations, to the retail sector and beyond.

Also consider this: Most militaries in the world operate without conscription. Modern militaries are on equal footing with businesses in recruiting men and women. Not surprisingly, labor market demographics have done the same thing for business that loss of conscription has done for the world's militaries. No one is compelled to work for you. It's your job to make the work experience attractive, interesting and career-enhancing.

In a military operation, careful planning is always essential for success. In business, recruiting in competitive (and sometimes downright hostile) environments takes careful planning and flexibility in executing a mission plan. If your organization is experiencing a recruiting problem, plan your mission, rally your troops (or what's left of them) and execute with vigor. You're preparing for your version of *Operation Talent Scout*. To succeed it must be an all-out team effort. If you fail to do this, you may find your organization in a weakened position. You may ultimately be outflanked (i.e., re-organized, purchased, merged or bankrupted) by a competitor.

Are you tired of fighting for good people? Is your team's performance a casualty of high turnover? Is it possible you're not experiencing a shortage of personnel but a shortage of skills? If you're open to new ways of recruiting talent for your organization, read on...

WANTED: A FEW GOOD MEN AND WOMEN

(preparing to fill a vacancy)

THE ECONOMIC EXPANSION of the last two decades is the longest peacetime expansion of the twentieth century. The nation's extraordinary financial performance has raised the question of whether the U.S. economy has entered a new age. A new age promises unprecedented increases in wealth and productivity. Yet it's a time hobbled with labor shortages. Attempting to locate, recruit and hire talented people is a formidable task. Unfavorable demographics predict a hiring crisis well into the next decade.

Long after the demand for Y2K with its drain on skills and resources has reached its peak, other "hot" skills will be needed by most all organizations. Making the perfect hiring decision poses challenges like never before. Are you ready to locate and recruit top candidates that are willing and able to adapt to a changing employment landscape?

If so, a job vacancy is an excellent opportunity to review the job function. Would a re-design of the job responsibilities be beneficial? For many companies, a sudden growth surge leads to the creation of new positions. Some of the positions will be needed indefinitely; others won't. You'll want to take time to identify long-range needs instead of hiring to "put out fires." It will help you contain costs. You owe it to yourself and your organization to take sufficient time to plan, develop and execute a recruiting strategy. Leaving it to chance can be disastrous.

For example, you may decide to hire some people for the long term but hire temporary or seasonal help for the short term. Contract employees are also in great demand, difficult to find and retain even for short-term projects. Regardless of what you're looking for, you'll need to plan for recruiting. You can get a head start by answering the questions in this chapter prior to beginning your search.

WHY DID THE LAST PERSON WHO HELD THIS JOB LEAVE?

Do you have the *true* answer to this question? Knowing why people leave is as important as knowing why they stay. If you don't know why people are leaving, you'll be hard-pressed to prevent it from happening again and again. Find out why your departing employees would rather work for someone else. It's possible that they're leaving because of interpersonal problems with their peers or immediate supervisor. Research indicates that those who don't get along with their supervisors are more likely to look for employment elsewhere.

Maybe they feel they're not being recognized enough for their hard work and the amount of time they spend on the job. Whatever the reasons, you need to know "why" if you want to keep your existing employees as well as hire people who will be a good fit for the future. Keep in mind that most people are motivated by money, but only to a point. Appreciation, opportunity for advancement, and a chance to learn new things are also key motivators and reasons why people stay.

In addition, if you're not currently conducting exit interviews, you may want to start. It's a good way to find out what's going on in the minds of the employees who have made the decision to quit. If you make it non-threatening and easy for them to be honest, you can learn a lot and hopefully avoid repeating past mistakes.

WHAT DOES MY TURNOVER REVEAL ABOUT THE KIND OF PERSON I SHOULD BE LOOKING FOR?

It's possible that the incumbent was a bad fit for the job from the beginning. Maybe he or she lacked some of the critical skills to do the work effectively and was unwilling or unable to learn (this is not as uncommon as one might believe).

On the other hand, you may have underestimated the amount of knowledge and prior work experience needed to perform the job. If you haven't done the job yourself, there are most likely some things that you're not familiar with which could lead to a miscalculation of the time, effort, skills and knowledge needed to do the work. It's also possible that the job changed and the employee was no longer qualified to handle the new responsibilities.

Whatever the reason, you have another chance to find someone to replace the individual who left. Know what you're looking for and why. Don't make a regrettable hiring decision because you need someone immediately and feel you can't wait to find the right person. "Warm bodies," those that are "barely breathing," are of little value in contributing to your bottom line. They can even cause more problems than you already have.

HAVE CHANGES BEEN MADE THAT MIGHT AFFECT MY HIRING DECISION?

Downsizing, rightsizing, re-engineering, mergers and buyouts can dramatically affect your department and the type of person you should hire. Even minor or perceived changes can impact employees and their attitudes about you, the job, the company and whether or not to start looking for another position either inside or outside the company.

With change may come a shift in personnel so that the type of person you're seeking now may be different than one that was a good fit three months ago. Consider past, present and future organizational changes and needs as you prepare to fill a vacancy. The only thing that is constant is change. Take into consideration the things that are taking place in your organization before you commit to hiring even one more person.

ARE MY EXPECTATIONS TOO HIGH?

Do you want too much from an employee? If you have more than six job requirements or minimum standards that a candidate must meet in order to be considered for a personal interview, you've screened out most of the population. Carefully screening, interviewing and hiring the best person for the job is a *must*, but if you're too picky, you may find yourself with chronic vacancies and unfinished work.

For example, some hiring managers automatically eliminate from consideration résumés and/or applications that contain spelling or grammatical errors. This sounds logical because attention to detail is important in most jobs. However, if writing skills aren't required for the job, you may have unnecessarily overlooked a favorable candidate that would be an excellent worker. A "diamond in the rough" with a great attitude may reward you with solid performance well into the future. Make a decision and start comparing applicants to your *specific job needs*.

SHOULD YOU RE-DEFINE THE JOB?

Before filling any position, review the job description. If possible, interview the incumbent about the job tasks. Decide whether or not the position description should be re-defined. Maybe the new hire will take on different responsibilities or even a completely new role. It's possible that you may want to change the job duties, reporting relationship, level of responsibility and degree of autonomy. This is the ideal time to make adjustments.

In writing a job description, start each job duty with an action verb similar to what you might find in an accomplishment statement on a résumé. Use short sentences with one idea per sentence. Don't try to include all of the details of the job. Job descriptions should offer an overview of what's required. It's an investment of time that can reap rewards when it's clear in your mind what you want and need from a new employee. It will help you as you interview candidates who may or may not be truly interested in doing the work you need done. It will provide clarification as you help the new employee get off to a good start on the new employee's first days, weeks and months at work.

DOES THE OPENING "NEED" TO BE FILLED?

Hiring managers are sometimes quick to fill a vacancy without much thought to whether or not it really *needs* to be filled. A job opening provides an opportunity to re-evaluate the workload and job functions. It's possible that the incumbent required eight hours to complete a job task that should have taken five. Maybe portions of the job could be shared among several employees. Perhaps some of the work could be eliminated all together. Sudden expansion or an increased workload often requires more help, but is it a long-term situation or would temporary employees be able to handle the work?

Evaluate the need before you hire. Get creative, especially if you require assistance only for the short-term. Too many people with not enough to do is not only financially foolish, but can lead to serious morale problems.

HOW MUCH "EXPERIENCE" IS REQUIRED?

Previous work experience is a "must" for many jobs. What you'll want to decide is *how much* in terms of months or years and what *type* of experience is needed to do the work you want done.

For example, in hiring an accounting manager would three years of experience be enough or would a minimum of five years be the least you would be willing to consider? Would this individual need previous experience in managing others? Would you require a minimum of having managed 10 people or would 50 be your minimum? The hiring manager is in the best position to make these decisions and should have the final say concerning who's selected.

As you consider experience, keep in mind that a candidate may claim five years of experience, but actually has only one year of experience repeated five times.

WHAT SPECIFIC "SKILLS" MUST THE NEW HIRE HAVE?

The more you know about what skills are needed or preferred to do the job, the easier it will be for you to quickly weed out the misfits. For example, if you were seeking someone with specific technical skills, would you consider applicants with fewer qualifications if you could teach them what they need to know? Or are there certain skills the candidates absolutely must have in order to perform the tasks you have in mind?

Although you may not find the person you want as quickly as you'd like, you'll know without question who would and wouldn't be a good fit because you took the time to decide what skills you value most.

WOULD I ACCEPT FEWER SKILLS IN LIEU OF "POTENTIAL?"

Potential has a lot to do with willingness to learn. Attitude is often more valuable than the skills themselves. If you hire people that are of average intelligence but who are motivated to learn, you can teach them most anything. However, if you make the mistake of hiring people that aren't committed to the task, potential means little or nothing. As you prepare to hire, evaluate candidates on what they already know and can do as well as their interest in and fit with future job opportunities within your organization.

HOW WILL I RECOGNIZE POTENTIAL?

The kinds of interview questions that you ask will help you recognize potential. Don't rely on gut feelings alone. Visceral reactions are important, but shouldn't be the only deciding factor when making a hiring decision. Some hiring managers have better intuition than others. To be safe, ask good questions and probe for clarification if you need more information. Ask behavior-based questions (discussed in Chapter 5). Look at "track records" of performance on the job. Personally check references; don't leave this important task to others.

The hiring manager is in the best position to determine whether or not what the references have to say makes sense. Selecting new hires based upon potential in some ways is a gamble. There's no guarantee a new hire will live up to potential, but a thorough screening and a review of past performance can help you decide whether to take a chance and make a job offer.

WHAT CAN I COMMIT IN RESOURCES?

You don't have to be a manager in a large corporation to recognize the value of education and training. The issue is how much are you willing and allowed to spend in educating your workforce? What type of additional training would be the most valuable? Are "soft" skills needed as much as technical or "hard" skills? How will you determine who will get to benefit from training opportunities? Will some people feel slighted because they're not selected?

In some companies, classroom learning is an incentive for doing a good job. Only those who meet or exceed their performance goals are invited to attend, for example, the annual employee educational conference. Although this may seem unusual or even de-motivating, it's an approach taken by some organizations to reward steady performers. Or maybe you have a different strategy and spend most of your training budget on the employees who need the most help, not your best performers. You're the one who can best decide what will work for you.

Additionally, do you offer a tuition assistance or reimbursement program? If so, are there any restrictions on what employees can and cannot study? Will the company pay only for classes that are related to the employee's work or will they pay for anything the employee wishes to pursue? Will you provide reimbursement for a certain portion of the tuition based on the grade the employee earns or will you pay for everything, regardless of the grade? Education is a big motivator for many people. Companies that fail to recognize its value often rob themselves of attracting and keeping top-notch people.

DO I NEED A SPECIALIST?

Sometimes hiring managers are seeking applicants with special skills when it's not necessary or likely the right person can be found. For example, you need an office manager for a medical clinic. You think you need someone who's a specialist in processing medical claims with insurance companies in addition to having experience with a variety of other tasks associated with a health care environment. After an exhaustive search, you haven't found anyone who meets your criteria as a specialist. But, you've had several applicants respond to your advertisement who have considerable work experience in office management. However, none of them have prior experience in a medical setting. Is it possible that an intelligent individual with broad-based experience and a willingness to learn could handle the job? If you're facing a labor shortage like many businesses are today, you might want to reconsider your "need" for a specialist.

WHAT'S MY MANAGEMENT STYLE?

Do you consider yourself a "no-nonsense" manager who rules with an iron fist? Are you a people-oriented leader, or are you strictly focused on the profits? Do you balance the needs of your employees with the need to make money?

Ideally, managers should spend roughly 85% of their time managing and leading people and only 15% on the details of the job. Oftentimes, that's not the case. Some managers over-manage, instead of lead and set the example. Others have no idea what their employees are doing; there's no structure or focus and people are confused which makes it almost impossible for them to do their best.

Furthermore, every manager has his or her individual approach to managing people and projects. For instance, if you give your current employees a substantial amount of freedom to make decisions, would a person who needs constant supervision be compatible with you and the rest of the team? If you need a strategic thinker, what would it be like to supervise someone who focuses on short-term rather than long-term goals? Some employees are at their best when working on immediate projects and tasks; others are not. You're the only one that can make the decision regarding your management style and the kind of person that best responds to you.

WHAT'S THE CULTURE LIKE HERE?

Every organization has a culture, as does every department within the organization. Is your culture formal or informal? Is it laissez-faire or highly structured? The diversity of the employees that make up your department also impacts the culture. Maybe you believe your employees "work hard and play hard." If that's the case, you'll want to hire people that share your same philosophy. Long hours aren't for everyone. Neither is extensive travel. Do your employees socialize with each other outside of work? Does the company encourage and support a ball team, company picnic and/or holiday party? Or is the company's philosophy "all business?"

For example, in one company, the vice-presidents and directors are required to wear suits to work while everyone else may wear "business casual." They don't associate with other employees nor do they attend company-sponsored functions that the "workers" attend. In another organization, the all-male executives have offices on a separate floor—segregated from the rest of the employees. Regardless of your culture, it's important to know what that culture is so that you can hire people that have the best chance for success.

WHO WILL BE MOST SUCCESSFUL?

This is an important question. It forms the foundation for your hiring strategy. It can also be a difficult question to answer. You might want to start by looking at the incumbent; how successful is that employee in the job? If a good fit, the incumbent can serve as a basis of comparison as you interview. If the incumbent is a misfit, you have an opportunity to find someone who's qualified and willing to do the job you have in mind.

In addition to the job requirements, list the qualities you're looking for in a candidate before you start recruiting. For example, are you seeking someone who's detail-oriented, gets along well with teammates and learns quickly? Most likely you are, as is your competition. If so, you won't discover this by reading a résumé or application. You'll have to conduct a thorough interview and carefully check references to learn more about a candidate's personal qualities.

In summary: The ability to make sound and defensible hiring decisions is often the wafer-thin difference between dedication, know-how and a willingness to take the right amount of time needed to get the job done effectively, not just rush to fill a space on the organizational chart. Furthermore, attracting and recruiting high quality people is the responsibility of everyone in the organization not just the hiring manager. Everyone who's employed by you has a stake in the future of the company. That future, whether exceptional or average, is dependent upon the team you hire.

As you prepare for your search, review the questions in this chapter. Write your answers down. Be sure you know what you want and need in your new hires before you rush to post a job opening, place an ad in the newspaper, advertise on the Internet or put a sign in front of your place of business.

Know what you're looking for and value in potential new employees. Then ask yourself: "Have I surveyed my current team for their ideas concerning what talents they would most appreciate in new co-workers? If not, why haven't I done this?" The people who currently work for you are an excellent resource when it comes to making hiring decisions that are the right choice for you and the rest of your employees. Get "buy-in" and valuable feedback by soliciting their opinions.

2

OPERATION TALENT SCOUT

(where and how to attract good people)

T HE AGING OF THE POPULATION and the impending retirement of the "baby boom" generation in the opening decades of the twenty-first century is a challenge facing both public and private sector employers. Technology has accelerated global communications and a need for people in most industries. Employees for marketing, distribution, sales, accounting, health care, information technology, etc., are all intertwined in an electronic universe in which the employee reigns. The challenges and opportunities that face modern-day employers in recruiting good people can't be taken lightly. It's a future of your choosing. Your options for recruiting personnel are numerous and multi-faceted.

It's no secret that one of the most important factors to a candidate is challenging and personally fulfilling work. The elimination of dress codes, allowing your employees to telecommute several days each week and compensatory time off can be reason for future employees to agree or not agree to accept an invitation for a job interview with you. Be prepared to discuss earning potential for the achievement of organizational as well as personal goals. Offer bonus opportunities or extra vacation days for outstanding performance. Promote education and allow your employees to attend company-sponsored seminars and conferences. Listen to your employees and don't just give them "lip service." These are some of the things that candidates are looking for in today's labor market. Know what you can and cannot offer. Then start your search for the people that are going to take your organization to the next level.

There are many methods for locating and recruiting your future staff. From working with agencies, to advertising in the newspaper, to referrals from current employees, the ideas are numerous and varied. Don't limit yourself to a handful of strategies unless you want to restrict your search.

This chapter contains ideas that have been used or are currently being used to find and enlist people for organizations of all types. Approach the hiring process with an open mind to new ways of recruiting, and have fun!

HERE ARE SOME SOURCES FOR FINDING THE NEXT SUPERSTARS FOR YOUR ORGANIZATION:

- Consider people that already report to you. Then search company-wide.

- Recruit seniors (over 50).

- Hold on-site job interviews.

- Contact job-lead organizations.

- Supply your employees with referral cards; reward your current employees with a bonus if their referral is hired.

- Your repeat customers know you. Maybe they'd like to work for you.

- Include your help-wanted ad in neighborhood coupon packages.

- Offer free "how to get a job" seminars through your local Chamber of Commerce.

- Be sure the receptionist and front office staff knows each applicant is to be treated like your best customer.

- Set-up a job hotline. Provide a 24-hour-a-day recorded message on your job hotline. People that call after hours can leave a name and phone number after listening to your pitch.

- Advertise for a first baseman, volleyball or basketball player. Include the statement: "By the way, you must be employed by our company to take part in the fun."

- Start an on-going *congratulations campaign* for local achievers—when a photo or article appears in the newspaper, mail a letter of application and say: "We're always interested in hiring successful people like you."

- Recruit from businesses that are laying-off or closing.

- Prepare for walk-ins. Make sure the work area is clean, windows are washed and yesterday's trash is removed. Be ready for them. Don't ask them to be seated while you complete petty tasks. A walk-in is usually a high-caliber, more motivated person than a phone caller.

- Recruit homemakers.

- Sponsor tailgate parties at college sporting events to recruit seasonal employees and future long-term employees.

- Take a closer look at prison parolees.

- Open facilities in geographic areas that workers prefer.

- Advertise the promise of an improved commute.

- Hold an open house for the community.

- Recruit at trade shows. Display a "help-wanted" sign in your booth.

- Hire people you may have rejected in the past such as people with disabilities or a history of welfare dependency.

- Advertise on college radio stations.

- Advertise with moving companies.

- Advertise using envelope stuffers.

- Advertise on billboards.

- Advertise on buses, trains, and rapid transit services.

- Send recruiters to home-and-garden shows. Many recent graduates attend such events as they're setting up housekeeping.

- Hire students in clerical and administrative positions in the hope they'll remain with the company after earning a degree.

- Find a company whose busy season comes at a different time than yours and swap employees.

- Include phrases such as "willing to train" or "no experience needed" in your classified advertisements.

- Develop and participate in school-to-work partnerships.

- Contact people after reading engagement and wedding announcements in newspapers. They often mention what kind of work the couples do. They may be interested in coming to work for you.

- Become an active member of your local high school's and/or technical school's work-study board.

- Recruit high school and college interns. Offer these same employees an incentive to hire on with you full time upon graduation.

- Work with college alumni associations.

- Recruit foreign exchange students for temporary work.

- Pair up with similar organizations to yours and "job share."

- Contact Newcomers' clubs.

- Make presentations to community organizations about what your company does.

- Recruit moonlighters.

- Recruit career-changers.

- Recruit retirees.

- Recruit retired or ex-military, including those about to separate from the service.

- Contact military reserve centers where technical skills abound.

- Contact former employees. They may not be happy with their decision to leave you, but are too embarrassed to ask to come back.

- Promote your company through local news stories.

- Look around the grocery store for people wearing T-shirts with competitors' logos or look for baseball hats with corporate logos at sporting events and talk to these people.

- Get creative with job postings. List the kinds of projects the employee will work on, the skills needed for each project and describe the training you'll provide for more challenging tasks.

- When you write classified ads, craft the copy to lead applicants to your Web site and/or e-mail address.

- Review the skills of your tenured staff. You're likely to find skills that can be quickly updated.

- Recruit on the Internet.

- Aggressively recruit passive recruits (people not actively seeking employment).

- Offer sign-on bonuses to new hires.

- Establish a hiring center decorated in a theme and schedule a fun event for new hires, such as a barbecue. Encourage new hires to bring anyone they know who could be a future employee.

- Allow managers to make on-the-spot job offers before paperwork and reference checks are completed.

- Pay applicants $25 to complete an application for employment. For some people getting started is the hardest part of looking for a job. Set limitations such as must be 21 years of age, have a valid driver's license, etc.

- Offer extras like free breakfast or free dinners for anyone working beyond regular hours.

- Offer bonuses for those who stay at least 6 months.

- Sponsor foreign workers for green cards.

- Contract with employment agencies. Let them do the leg-work for you.

- Advertise with the Department of Labor.

- Pay people from outside the company for referrals that you hire.

- Hire the mentally and physically challenged.

- Take a harder look at people with various backgrounds, cultures and language proficiency.

- Scour Web pages and association rosters for people who could be good job candidates.

- Ask candidates what would make working for you a "dream job?" Then comply if you hire the person.

- Interview exiting part-time and full time workers to see if a counter-offer might reverse their decision to leave.

- Take business cards from restaurant fish bowls.

- Spam every user of a chat room about a job vacancy.

- Build a game or puzzle on your company Web site. Then offer every solver an interview or a job.

- Offer "notification" bonuses to current employees that disclose a competitor's attempt to woo them away.

- Terminate your worst managers and supervisors. Bad bosses are often the reason well-regarded employees quit and prospective new employees have no interest in working for you.

- Widen your search. Include people who in the past were not targeted during your recruiting.

- Be willing to accept less or do without until you can find someone you can live with.

  In summary: We're in a time of labor shortages that aren't predicted to abate in the near future. Business demands require employers to do one of two things: you can either continue to recruit job hoppers, pay higher and higher salaries and create an environment of more, more, more. Or you selectively recruit to hire top talent and foster a work environment where people are committed to stay for the long haul. It all starts with finding and attracting the people who most closely meet your job requirements.

  Be aware that by the year 2050 the U.S. population is expected to increase by 50 percent, with immigration accounting for almost two-thirds of that growth. About half of Americans will belong to what is now considered minority groups, compared with slightly more than a quarter today. These demographic changes will challenge managers to find and keep good people. It could get to the point where companies won't be able to grow as fast as they want to because they won't have enough people to make that happen.

Don't lower your standards. Hiring marginal candidates leads to firing marginal employees. Take the time to develop your plan; don't be afraid to get creative in your search efforts. Once you've found the right people for the job, think about employing strategies for keeping them challenged and motivated.

Employers in offices and factories alike need to recognize that the fear of downsizing, loss of job security and the stress associated with overwhelming changes in technology will affect employee retention statistics. Employees need managers who empathize with their pain and who honestly try to create an environment in which everyone is respected and feels valued.

*Joseph Daniel McCool, editor of **Recruiting Trends**, a monthly publication based in New Hampshire summed it up:*

"Your ability to grow as a company is tied to your ability to tell your company's story and convince people to work there."

THEY CAN'T FOOL THE OFFICERS, OR CAN THEY?

(screening applications and résumés)

E VERY HIRING MANAGER needs a method for quickly screening résumés and applications; both offer clues about the candidates. Applications are generally completed prior to the first meeting with the interviewer. Some companies require applicants to complete the application on-site while others may permit applicants to take it home. Regardless of how you collect applications, you can eliminate approximately fifty percent of those who apply by pre-screening applications and résumés.

A résumé is the job seeker's calling card and its purpose is to get the job interview. The applicant decides what to include on the résumé and what to eliminate. It's up to you to decipher what it all means; this can sometimes be difficult. Remember that many job seekers get professional advice on how to create and structure a résumé. They will share what they want you to see and little more.

Therefore, most résumés include only the candidates' most significant accomplishments. Keep in mind that some candidates are better at presenting themselves on paper than others. Look for communication style, inconsistencies, and anything that might create questions in your mind regarding the candidate's skills, knowledge, experience, education and overall talent. Decide whether or not you'll eliminate a candidate from further consideration because of what you see on a résumé or application.

AS YOU SCREEN RÉSUMÉS ASK YOURSELF:

- If there's a career objective, is it specific or general?

- Does the résumé include statements citing qualifications resulting in significant accomplishments, or is it merely a string of job descriptions?

- Is a stated accomplishment too good to be true? This would be important to check out in the interview.

- Did the author start each sentence with action verbs that clearly convey thoughts that grab your attention?

- Is the résumé more than two pages in length?

- Are the words crowded together, or is there enough white space to make it easy to read?

- Do the dates and sequence of events that apply to education, training, and work experience make sense?

- Is the résumé understandable?

- How willing are you to forgive spelling and grammatical errors?

- Does the résumé succeed in getting the author's message across?

Every manager needs a method that allows for quick and reliable screening of applications. The information on an application is usually straightforward and devoid of the embellishment that a résumé provides and it's therefore easier to spot deficiencies and inconsistencies.

AS YOU SCREEN APPLICATIONS ASK YOURSELF:

- Are there blank spaces on the application that you expected the candidate to complete? Blank spaces could mean they have something to hide or don't pay attention to detail.

- Are there unexplained gaps in the work history?

- Does the applicant's reason for leaving a previous job concern you?

- Are dates of work experience and education consistent?

- If your application asks for references, are they listed?

- Are references immediate supervisors, or are they other individuals who did not directly supervise the applicant? Not listing immediate supervisors could mean the applicant has trouble getting along with people or has something to hide.

- Did the applicant follow instructions in completing the application?

- Is the completed application form neat and without strikeouts, ink smudges or food/beverage stains? Messy applications typically translate into sloppy work.

REMAIN IMPARTIAL

Screening résumés and applications can be a challenge, especially if you receive hundreds or even thousands in a month's time, as do some organizations. But even if you have only a few from which to decide which candidates are worthy of a personal interview, the key is to remain impartial. You'll want to screen résumés against your specific job requirements. It's the best way to remain objective. Screen with a yellow highlighter and mark anything that's unclear and needs further explanation. Credentials are essential ingredients that go into making a good hiring decision.

In a real-life example, an applicant was chosen for a personal interview because she indicated fluency in Russian on her résumé. She was offered a job because the hiring manager decided that because she spoke Russian, she could learn to handle difficult questions at a call center's busy help desk. However, the new hire failed to meet the minimum requirements of the job as well as the manager's expectations. She was asked to leave shortly thereafter. Her ability to speak a foreign language had nothing to do with her ability to handle the job for which she was hired. The hiring manager falsely believed that because she could speak Russian she could learn how to do anything. He was wrong.

THERE'S AN ADVANTAGE TO EMPLOYMENT APPLICATIONS

Most organizations require job seekers to fill out an application for employment because it requires a signature and is a legally binding document. Applications are usually completed prior to the first meeting with the employer. Some companies will mail application forms to applicants upon request. Others have a policy that all applications must be completed at the employment site. That way there's no doubt about who completed the form. Mistakes, sloppiness and inconsistencies can be attributed to the applicant and taken into consideration when evaluating the individual as a potential new hire.

Employment applications often contain a statement such as: "I understand that false or misleading information may result in termination of employment." Applicants are asked to sign the statement and therefore agree to termination if found lying or providing bad information.

APPLICATIONS SHOULDN'T VIOLATE EMPLOYMENT LAWS

Your company's choice of an employment application may be out of your control. However, if you see something that's questionable, bring it to the attention of your human resources department or manager in charge. For example, some applications ask for date of birth or date graduated from elementary school and/or high school. Asking for this information is in violation of the law. In addition, your application may not ask any of the following questions although this list is not all-inclusive:

- Do you rent or own your home?

- Who resides with you?

- How long have you lived in the United States?

- How old are you?

- What is your date of birth?

- Are you over the age of 40?

- Where were you born?

- Where were your parents, spouse, and/or other relatives born?

- Are you a U.S. citizen?

- Are you male or female?

- What is your marital status?

- What is your race?

- What is your religion?

- What are your religious holidays?

- Have you ever been arrested?

- Do you plan to have children?

- How many children do you have?

- How old are your children?

- Who takes care of your children while you're working?

- Are you pregnant?

- Questions regarding military service such as date and type of discharge.

- Questions regarding service in a foreign military.

- Questions regarding the applicant's current or past assets or liabilities or credit rating including bankruptcy or garnishment.

- Any questions regarding the applicant's health.

- Requesting that the applicant affix a photograph to the application.

- Requesting a photo after the interview but before employment begins.

WHEN EVALUATING A COVER LETTER ASK YOURSELF:

- Is it an *original* letter?

- Is the salutation personalized?

- Does it show insight into your organization?

- Is it clear, clean and visually appealing?

- Is it well-organized?

- Is it written concisely?

- Does it get your attention and sell you on the applicant?

READ BETWEEN THE LINES WHEN READING COVER LETTERS

Most job seekers will enclose a cover letter with their résumé. Cover letters often reveal as much as the résumé itself. Yet many managers don't read the cover letter or know how to evaluate what they read. Learn how to read "between the lines" and get additional clues about the candidate. The salutation immediately tells you about the candidate's level of sophistication. Sharp candidates will make it a point to try to find out to whom they're sending the cover letter and résumé. They'll personalize the cover letter by addressing the receiver by name (e.g., "Dear Mr. Jones").

Beyond the salutation, a good cover letter will mention the company's specific requirements as mentioned in the classified ad, as told by a recruiter or as revealed by some other source and the candidate's strengths as they relate to those needs. If you've asked for salary requirements in your advertisement, the applicant might also include that information, but don't be surprised if your request is ignored. Savvy job seekers know that salary information is used to screen people out. They may therefore fail to include it and take a chance you may be interested in them anyway.

BEWARE OF "YELLOW FLAGS"

"Yellow Flags" are cautionary and may indicate that a problem exists. But don't use them to disqualify candidates prematurely. As recently as ten years ago "Yellow Flags" often eliminated applicants who today would be acceptable due to the labor shortage. When screening applications and résumés, you may want to consider gaps or regression in work history, many jobs in a short period of time and reasons for leaving. Yet it can be dangerous to take everything on a résumé or application at face value because it's relatively easy for the applicant to falsify information.

Research suggests that almost one-half of all job seekers lie, distort, or in some way fabricate information and that more than half a million people in the United States claim bogus degrees. However, automatically eliminating a candidate based solely on unsubstantiated warnings could rob you of a talented new team member.

Some of the "Yellow Flag" warnings in addition to those items mentioned previously in this section for résumés and applications include:

- Salary inconsistencies.

- Vague answers. Examples:

  1. Listing a city or state of a former employer but not the complete address.

  2. Reasons for leaving former employers.

  3. Unusual response to the question, "Have you ever been convicted of a felony?"

- Regression in job responsibilities and job title.

- What appears to be inflated credentials.

Examples:

1. Inflating degrees (Associate Degree versus a Bachelor of Science Degree).

2. Inflating graduating status (Magna Cum Laude or Phi Beta Kappa).

- Degree earned but no institution listed.

- Qualifiers such as:

1. "Had exposure to."

2. "Have knowledge of."

3. "Assisted with."

4. "Worked with."

- Includes the word "attended" with regard to a school in the hope that you may not recognize that they did not graduate.

- Frequent job changes. (Use care when evaluating this as certain high tech workers go from project to project rather quickly).

- More than one reference that is "out of business."

Make a decision on whether or not to invite the candidate for a personal interview based on the information provided. Note the things that concern you and ask about them in a preliminary telephone interview.

APPLICANTS PLAY DOWN WEAKNESSES

You can't blame job seekers for trying to impress you. Most people want you to know what they have to offer and how well they've worked in the past. They'll hide their short-comings and unless you ask, are not likely to reveal a poor attitude, problem with performance or conflict with a previous supervisor. It's up to the interviewer to find out what the applicant is really like. The best way to find out is through the interview. However, don't let it become an interrogation. Listen carefully to what's being said; watch body language and "hear" what the applicant is *not* saying.

Conversely, some job seekers are too modest; you'll need to discover their skills and experience with interview questions that draw them out of their shyness. Then make a decision based upon what you hear.

> *In summary: Take the time to carefully review résumés and applications. It will save you valuable time in the long run. Despite the fact that some applicants use professional services to prepare their résumés, many don't. Even if they do, that doesn't mean that you can't gather valuable information from reading them. Résumés, applications and cover letters generally offer insight into an applicant's qualifications providing you know how to interpret the data.*

"Never judge a book by its cover" is a cliché, yet it holds true with applications and résumés. There may be good reason for what appears to be discrepancies in documents. It's your job to find out more through a series of questions during the telephone interview. Decide then whether to invest additional time in the candidate with a face-to-face meeting.

The strength of the U.S. economy provides a remarkable opportunity for most organizations to focus on a bright future. The key to the long-term financial health of your enterprise is being able to identify and hire successive generations of people who share your commitment for high achievement and profitability. Résumés and applications are an essential part of the recruiting process. Learn how to use the information they provide to your best advantage.

NOW HEAR THIS

(telephone screening)

P RE-SCREENING CANDIDATES by telephone can save you time and money. Yet it's a step in the hiring process that's frequently overlooked. It provides an opportunity to quickly find out more about the candidate and confirm and question information that appears on the résumé and/or application. It's also a quick barometer to measure a candidate's interest in working for you.

Don't try to trick or pressure a candidate on the telephone. Some managers are under the mistaken impression that by asking inappropriate questions they'll learn more about the prospective new hire. In reality, they run the risk of being accused of discrimination as well as being rejected by a candidate who doesn't have time for "games."

By the end of the telephone interview you'll have gathered information that includes:

- The candidate's knowledge of your organization.

- How closely the candidate "fits" the profile with the résumé/application in terms of do they or do they not have the credentials they claim they have?

- How well the candidate communicates verbally.

- How well the candidate can sell him or herself to you by telephone.

- Whether or not the candidate has a good sense of humor.

- A measurement of "chemistry" between you and the candidate.

- Whether it makes sense to invest more time in a personal interview.

You can obtain quite a bit of information with only a few questions. Phone screening also gives you an opportunity to be objective. Physical appearance and age are inconsequential when you can't see the candidate. It's a good chance to evaluate people based on answers to your questions, not physical attributes, which often create an immediate and unjust bias in the mind of the interviewer. Whether you're hiring someone to fly commercial airplanes, or someone to run your quality control department, evaluate people on their qualifications. Successful organizations must rely on brainpower and not outward appearances in selecting new employees.

BE UPBEAT AND FRIENDLY

The best way to help candidates feel comfortable and "sell" your company and the job at the same time is to be cordial and positive. The by-product of your efforts is typically people who are willing to share information about themselves. The more you know about candidates and their motives for wanting to work for you, the better your chances for hiring the right people for your department.

QUESTION INCONSISTENCIES

Don't hesitate to probe for further understanding, especially when the candidate is inconsistent in what's said or what's said in contrast to the résumé and/or application. For instance, if a candidate says in the interview that she has four years of experience in retail sales as a manager, but her résumé indicates only two years, you have a right to ask for more information.

In another example, if a candidate indicates on an application that he has worked as a budget analyst, but is unable to support that statement in a personal interview, question him further. It's possible you misunderstood; it's also possible that he's trying to trick you into believing he has experience in a field where he only worked for a short time and knows relatively little.

DON'T MAKE PROMISES YOU CAN'T KEEP

In an effort to entice candidates to join your operation, you may be tempted to offer more than you can give. Suggesting that the new employee will have an office with a view versus a six by six cubicle would be a mistake. Telling a candidate that a bonus is part of the package when in fact, most employees never earn one, will soon be discovered. Trying to fool someone into believing that the work environment is not stressful when in reality it's just the opposite is unethical and will be determined quickly by your new employee. In short, don't make promises you can't keep; the end result could be disastrous and you most likely will lose the employee anyway.

CONCLUDE BY TELLING THE CANDIDATE WHAT HAPPENS NEXT

It's not only impolite to leave a candidate "hanging," but it's bad business. Candidates are naturally interested in what you think about them after the telephone interview. You're not obligated, nor do I suggest that you give immediate feedback especially if it's unfavorable. However, it's a good idea to let candidates know that you'll be in contact one way or the other.

If you decide you're not interested in the individual you just interviewed, it would be best to send a letter that simply says: "Thank you for taking the time to interview with our company. We have selected another candidate for the position." That's all you need to say. In fact, to say more could create some problems if the candidate challenges your reason for rejection and you can't support it.

USE A SYSTEM FOR EVALUATING CANDIDATES

When you finish screening you'll want to immediately complete an evaluation form. If you wait until you've spoken to several candidates before documenting your thoughts, you may forget what you heard or get confused. Try to remain unbiased and hear not only what you want to hear. Record the *facts* using complete sentences. Focus on how well the candidates match your specific job requirements. Don't write anything that could be viewed as discriminatory.

> **In summary:** *Telephone screening can be an effective use of your time providing you use a list of pre-planned questions to help you stay focused. If you're at a loss for what to ask, check out* **Hiring Top Performers-350 Great Interview Questions For People Who Need People**, *one of my other books which lists questions in 8 categories that will help you decide what to ask while staying within the law.*

> *Build rapport by making the candidate feel at ease. Be friendly and positive. Gather enough information so that you can make a decision regarding whether or not to invite*

the candidate to meet with you in person. Don't eliminate anyone based on "Yellow Flag" warnings, as they are only warnings, and can be misleading. Some of your best employees may be people who didn't impress you upon your first encounter.

Conclude the interview by telling the interviewee what happens next. It's good business etiquette and even if you're not interested in hiring the individual at this time you may have a need later. Your reputation as a manager and that of your company is important. Good manners are always in vogue. A bit of the "golden rule" is applicable here. Don't leave applicants wondering whether or not they will hear from you again. We've all been on the other side of the desk at some point in our careers; don't forget what that was like. Your follow up is a reflection on you as well as your organization.

5

ATTENTION ON DECK

(effective interviewing)

INTERVIEWING IS A SKILL that can be learned. But organizations that don't educate their managers often see them hire for the wrong reasons and end up with employees that are a bad fit for the job and the company. Many people hire only those people they think are like themselves. However, to do so can be a mistake because a diverse workforce can add tremendous value to the organization.

Asking the right questions helps to insure legally compliant interviews. Good questions will keep you focused and help control the discussion. The best questions are probing and require that the candidate explain the "who," "what," "when," "where," "why," and "how" of their skills and work experience. Candidates can easily answer the "what" questions. But the "how" questions require candidates to explain in detail how they did something. If they haven't done it, they won't be able to fake it. It's nearly impossible to answer the "how" question and show depth and knowledge without having performed the task.

Some managers hire purely on "gut feelings" or intuition. That can also lead to disastrous results. They both play a role in the hiring process, but should be used as a confirmation after a series of pre-planned questions are asked during the interview. Beyond the questioning, hire for attitude, everything else is secondary, and then if necessary, train for required skills. There's a prophetic axiom that applies here:

> *"People are hired for aptitude and fired for attitude."*

Don't let it happen to you by overlooking the value of a positive attitude.

Because of the keen competition for talent, recruiting and hiring people who are open to training may be your best strategy. It's important to note that many companies grow their own talent through training. This may be an option for you if you aren't already doing so.

PREPARE FOR THE INTERVIEW

You run the risk of perpetuating past hiring mistakes by not preparing for the interview. It's your responsibility as a manager and that of your team to make sure that you're ready to meet the candidates. The feelings the candidates leave with when the interview is over will impact their decision to accept or reject your job offer. Even if you don't make a job offer, you've left an impression that could be good or bad, depending upon what took place. In a well-planned interview you should be able to learn enough about a candidate to make a sound and defensible choice.

Prepare for the interview by defining what you're looking for in a candidate in terms of work experience, skills, education and/or certification. Then decide what you want to know and make a list of questions you plan to ask. Develop your agenda, start the interview on time, and stay within your time constraints. Resist the temptation to get off on a tangent either through your doing or that of the candidate. Sometimes we hear something "interesting" but it has nothing to do with the candidate's fit for the job. Don't waste valuable time on trivia or unrelated dialogue.

MEET AND GREET

Greet the candidate in person and you'll send the message that what's about to take place is important enough for you, the hiring manager, to personally greet and escort the candidate to the place where the interview will be held. Never send a messenger or another staff member to handle this important task. In addition, many people have unusual first and/or last names. Make sure you know how to pronounce the name of the candidate; it's an important part of the rapport-building process.

ESTABLISH RAPPORT

Candidates are more likely to share their weaknesses as well as their strengths if they see you as friendly and non-threatening. In addition, candidates are evaluating your work environment. If they feel that people aren't friendly, most likely they won't be interested in working for you. Keep in mind that they're leaving a job, in many cases, where they feel comfortable with the familiar people and things that surround them. If you give them the impression that your organization is not a congenial, happy and fun place to work, you may lose an excellent candidate to the competition.

In addition, a genuine smile is a powerful door opener. Most people probably don't smile enough, yet a smile can quickly reduce the miles between you and a stranger that has come to interview with you for a job. It takes 34 muscles to frown while it takes only 17 to smile!

Don't forget a firm handshake; it conveys a message of welcome. Start with small talk and then briefly explain the purpose of the interview. You can maintain control of the interview this way and run less of a risk that the candidate will try to take over.

Share your agenda. Then say:

> *"I'd like to ask you some questions. When I'm finished feel free to ask me anything you'd like to ask."*

Treat your candidates just as you would guests in your home. Be sure they're comfortable. Offer coffee, water or a soft drink. Make sure they know where the restroom is if they're going to be with you for any length of time. Provide lunch or dinner if appropriate.

Be prepared to answer their questions at the end of the interview.

AVOID OFF-THE-CUFF INTERVIEWS

Some inexperienced hiring managers believe that impro vised, spontaneous or casual interviews are the best kind. In reality, they can lead to poor hiring decisions. Learn how to structure interview questions (*See Appendix for sample questions*). Practice role-playing with a colleague. Assume the role of the interviewer. If you get an answer that's confusing or inconsistent, ask for clarification. You have a right to probe for additional information with job-related questions until you're satisfied with what you've heard.

GET TO THE POINT

The candidate's time is as valuable as yours. Don't keep the candidate waiting. To do so sends the message that your meeting isn't important. Begin with small talk; it's a great way to start the interview and help the candidate relax. But don't over do it and waste valuable time with too much casual conversation. You have a limited amount of time in which to find out if the candidate would be a good addition to your team. Follow your agenda and stick to your list of questions; it's the best way to compare candidates against one another and it will help you stay focused.

INTERVIEW FOR RETENTION

Part of the hiring manager's job is to sound out the interviewee for a sense of what he or she is looking for in a job. If a new hire is able to answer, "yes" to the following questions several months later, the applicant is probably going to be a good fit.

- Am I being fairly compensated?

- Am I getting enough opportunity to learn new things?

- Am I being challenged in my work?

- Do I fit in with the rest of the team members?

- Do I feel like I have a "future" with this organization?

- Has my supervisor been fair and honest with me?

- Do I have the authority needed to carry out my responsibilities?

- Do I get enough honest feedback from my immediate supervisor?

- Am I working a reasonable amount of hours or am I on my way to job burnout?

EXPLAIN WHAT YOU DO

Start the interview by explaining what you do and how your job relates to the position for which he or she is interviewing. However, be careful that you don't give away too much information, or you run the risk that you won't get an accurate picture of the candidate. Many candidates are carefully coached to interview well. Those who are clever will get you talking. They'll ask questions and when it's their turn to answer your questions, they'll tell you exactly what you want to hear. It's an old trick that many inexperienced hiring managers fall for.

AVOID STRESS TACTICS

Stress tactics reveal little about how a candidate will act in a real-life situation. Seating a candidate in a chair with one leg shorter than the rest, or asking a question such as:

> *"If you were a tree, what kind of tree would you be?"*

puts the candidate on the defensive. Contrary to what some people believe, creating artificial stressors won't give you a realistic picture of how someone will react under pressure in an actual situation.

> ***In a true example, a woman shared this story:*** *"I arrived at the interview and was very nervous. I was escorted to the interviewer's office where I sat down. As the ques-*

*tioning started, I realized the interviewer had
ants crawling up the legs of her desk. They
soon covered the surface of the desk and
without saying anything to me she started
squishing them with her index finger. This
went on throughout the thirty-minute interview. I was aghast! I couldn't concentrate. I
blew the interview! I didn't get the job offer
and felt bad because I really wanted the
job."*

The candidate would have been an excellent employee
but whether intentional or unintentional, the stress of the
ants cost the interviewer a talented future staff member.

TREAT CANDIDATES LIKE YOUR BEST CUSTOMERS

As simple as this principle may sound, many hiring managers fail to recognize the value of an exceptionally positive
meeting with candidates. Treat them like royalty; it's the
best way to sell what you have to offer. Focus on keeping
them comfortable, both physically and mentally.

In addition, be sure the candidate has enough "stretch
breaks" if spending the day at your company. Make it clear
that you're paying for the meal to avoid embarrassment on
the candidate's behalf. When candidates depart, it should be
with positive thoughts and a desire to work for you. And
even if you decide not to offer the job, you'll want them to
walk away with good feelings about you and your organiza-

tion. Who knows, some day they could be one of your best customers.

USE A PRE-PLANNED SERIES OF QUESTIONS

Questions help gain information about the candidate's knowledge, skills and qualities. The key here is "preplanned." In order to get the most from an interview you'll want to decide what questions you want to ask and why and in what order. If you have a team of people participating in the interview process they'll also need to be prepared. Asking questions from your list will help you stay focused and keep you out of legal hot water.

It's relatively easy to determine whether or not a candidate has the skills and work experience to do the job. The challenge is determining whether or not the individual has the traits and qualities to interface effectively with peers, customers, vendors and supervision. The number one reason for turnover is conflict with the immediate supervisor. You can avoid problems by hiring people who fit in with the rest of your team from day one.

ASK BEHAVIOR-BASED QUESTIONS

Behavior-based questions require the candidate to provide specific information about past performance and behavior. It's the best way to find out if the candidate is able and willing to do the things that you need done. By asking an individual to describe the past by sharing a real-life example with you in the interview, you can get a good sense of maturity and degree of accomplishment.

A hypothetical question on the other hand, gives the applicant the opportunity to lie and more or less tell you anything he or she wants to tell you. You may decide to use a combination of hypothetical and behavior-based questions. Just be aware that behavior-based questions are more effective in helping you gain information.

Numerous studies suggest that people tend to repeat past performance and that the more recent the past the more likely they'll behave in the same manner in the future. For that reason try asking some of the following behavior-based questions:

- Can you give me an example of a time when you "broke the rules?"

- How have you enlisted the help of teammates in solving a problem?

- How have you used your position as a leader to get what you want?

- Tell me about a time when you had to be especially tactful when handling a sensitive situation.

- Tell me about the worst decision you made in your last job.

- Can you give me an example of a recurring problem that you failed to solve?

- Tell me about a tough decision that you had to make in your prior position.

Each of these questions forces the candidate to think about the past and provide an example that will give you insight into future performance and behavior. They are tough questions to answer but tend to yield valuable information.

FOCUS ON THE MOST IMPORTANT QUESTIONS FIRST

Nothing contributes more to a candidate's value than his or her work experience doing the work you need done or experiences that easily transfer. Start the interview with small talk. Then ease into questions related to the work experience and skills that you want to explore. If you have a complete understanding of the job, you should have no trouble determining if the candidate meets your requirements providing you ask good questions. Once you've determined compatibility in these two areas, you'll want to get a feel for the candidate's personality and how he or she will blend in with the rest of your employees.

EDUCATION IS GENERALLY LESS IMPORTANT THAN WORK EXPERIENCE

It's the difference between knowing what something is or knowing how to do something and actually doing it. Today's managers are focusing more on skills and experience than whether or not the candidate has a degree, diploma or certificate.

Decide how much education and training you feel is necessary. You may also want to consider the type and amount of training you're prepared to offer the new hire once he or she joins your organization. An employee that's short on formal education, but has the interest and ability to learn, can be as valuable as an individual with a degree and no on-the-job experience.

DON'T TALK TOO MUCH

In an effort to sell the company and the job, many hiring managers talk and talk and talk. Call it a "hard sell" if you like. It's usually a poor attempt at trying to convince the candidate to work for you. However, when you talk too much you don't give the candidate time to sell himself to you. You also run the risk that you'll share so much information that the candidate will tell you exactly what you want to hear. When that happens, you risk sacrificing a realistic picture of the candidate's strengths and weaknesses. So how much should you talk?

Follow the *80/20 Rule*. Spend 80 percent of your time listening and 20 percent explaining the job and discussing the company and benefits of working for you. However, you'll want to wait until the end of the interview to do this.

CONTROL THE INTERVIEW

The more the candidate talks, the more control you have over the interview. When you're doing the questioning, you're in charge. When the tables are turned and the candidate starts questioning you, especially at the beginning of the interview, you're in trouble if you don't regain control. Inexperienced hiring managers sometimes allow that to happen and then wonder why they don't get an honest picture of the candidate.

Should the candidates try to take control, redirect the conversation by saying:

> *"I'd be happy to answer your questions after I've had the opportunity to question you."*

However, be careful that you're sensitive to the candidates and how they respond to your suggestion. You don't want to alienate a possible contender because you appear to be unwilling to answer questions. The hiring manager is in the best position to determine the most effective approach to questioning during the interview. You'll want to answer questions, but not before you gather enough information to decide whether or not you want to invite the candidate back for a second interview.

DETERMINE WEAKNESSES

Many hiring managers concentrate on the candidate's strengths. What a candidate has to offer is very important and you can bet that those who are prepared for the interview will be quick to tell you what they do well. However, if you can find out where a candidate is weak (we all have weaknesses) you'll know immediately whether or not the individual is the person for whom you're looking.

Some of the questions you may want to ask that will help you determine weaknesses are:

- Can you tell me about the last time you lost your temper at work?

- Tell me about a time when you got into a disagreement with your supervisor.

- Give an example of a time when you were disappointed in your work performance.

- Tell me about a time when you found it difficult to stay motivated.

- We all have weaknesses; please share with me two that you're working on to improve.

- Tell me about a time when your supervisor criticized you.

TAKE THE CANDIDATE'S NON-VERBAL GESTURES WITH A GRAIN OF SALT

There's a lot of controversy over interpretation of "body language." Even the experts can easily misjudge gestures, body position and facial expressions. When you judge a candidate based on raised eyebrows, crossed arms or an expressionless face, you could be cheating yourself out of an excellent future employee. There are many interpretations of non-verbal communication that may or may not have anything to do with what you think they mean.

> *For example: A candidate that's tired because he was up during the night caring for a sick child may appear disinterested or bored when in reality he's simply tired. A candidate with legs crossed may be trying to ease lower back pain, not sub-consciously communicating an unwillingness to listen or be open to your ideas. A candidate with poor eye contact may be nervous. Many candidates are nervous, as are some interviewers. Think twice before eliminating a candidate strictly based on non-verbal communication; it could be a costly mistake.*

AVOID AN INQUISITION

Some hiring managers get so intense when asking questions that the candidates feel like they're in front of a firing squad. Avoid this type of questioning by taking time to build rapport with the candidate. Don't think of the interview as just an interview. The more comfortable you make the candidate feel the better your chances for learning what you want to know. Put yourself in the candidate's place. How would you feel if you were invited for an interview and were bombarded with questions and you barely had time to catch your breath? It's not fun and not a good way to help the candidate relax either.

DON'T ASK LEADING QUESTIONS

When you ask a question such as:

> *"You're proficient in Microsoft Project, aren't you?"*

you signal the candidate that you're looking for a certain answer. Whether or not he's competent or experienced, you offer him a chance to tell you exactly what you want to hear. What you're hoping for may not be the case, but the candidate may be hesitant to disappoint you and decide to stretch the truth. If you find yourself in this situation after asking a question like this one, probe for further clarification. Better yet, avoid leading questions altogether.

GIVE CANDIDATES AN OPPORTUNITY TO EXPLAIN DISCREPANCIES

The old expression, "don't judge a book by its cover," (mentioned in Chapter 3) also applies to candidates and how you judge them. It's human nature to make decisions about people based on how they look and what they say and do. You may encounter a great candidate, but find something about her that doesn't seem "right."

For example: *The candidate tells you that she worked in the accounting department of a large firm. However, her application for employment doesn't reflect that experience. Before you eliminate her from further consideration, explore the discrepancies with the candidate. Don't be afraid to ask questions. There could be a mistake on the application. There could also be a good reason for what was presented in writing versus what the individual said in a personal interview.*

KNOW WHAT A "SUCCESSFUL" RESPONSE IS

A candidate's successful response will answer the question to your satisfaction. The response should also be to the point and provide you with further insight into the candidate's work experience and skills. Concentrate on what the answer reveals about the candidate's honesty, values, beliefs, personality and work ethic as these things are as important as anything you could learn about the candidate's technical skills.

LISTEN FOR WHAT THE CANDIDATE MAY BE HIDING

You ask a question and you get an evasive response. The candidate may be telling you something significant without saying anything or by saying something that has little or nothing to do with what you asked. Listen carefully. You may learn more about candidates by what they're *not* saying.

If you find yourself interviewing a candidate that seems to be concealing something, don't give up. Keep asking, probing and challenging until you feel you have the information you need to make a judgment regarding the viability of the candidate for your organization.

MANY CANDIDATES HAVE BEEN COACHED

What do you do when every answer you hear seems to be the "right answer?" Probe deeper to determine if the candidate can really do what's claimed. Don't be fooled by the smooth talker who seems to be exactly what you're looking for, the type of person who shines in the interview, but quickly tarnishes once hired.

On the other hand, there are some candidates who appear to be too good to be true but are actually excellent employees. Some of these people are overlooked because employers can't accept the fact that they're as good as they seem. Some appear to be over-qualified. Hiring the right people gets down to whether or not the person you're interviewing meets your needs. If the answer is "yes," and you can honestly say to yourself, "I've done a thorough job of interviewing and checking references," then it's time to make a job offer. Don't waste time in doing so if you found the person you want. Good people are often lost because of hiring managers who take too long to make up their minds.

DON'T GET FOOLED BY
AN INTERVIEWING PHENOMENON
CALLED "RECENCY"

"Recency" is when the individual *currently* being interviewed appears to be the best fit. To get maximum benefit from your search and interview efforts, don't get to a point where the last or most recent candidate interviewed gets the job offer because he or she is foremost in your mind. If you've made a commitment to interview several candidates, stick to your plan so you have a basis for comparison. In addition, you may need a "second choice" if your first choice rejects your offer.

Research supports the idea that the last person interviewed is three times more likely to be hired than the first person interviewed. Many people who are responsible for making hiring decisions don't have a system. Without a method for comparing candidates against one another, it's easy to make wrong choices and choose the last person who seemed acceptable.

In a real-life example, a business owner had four candidates to choose from that were presented to him by a retained search firm. Each of the four finalists was equally qualified to assume the role of the new member of the team. The owner was to spend one day with each of the four candidates. After the first day, he thought he had found his future employee. But he knew he had to honor his commitment to interview the other three. The second candidate was more impressive than the first and he was ready to make her a job offer. By the end of the fourth day he knew his choice was actually number three. Had he stopped interviewing and offered the job to the first person interviewed, he wouldn't have hired the best person for the job.

The moral of the story: don't let your mind trick you into believing that the candidate in front of you is necessarily "the one." You owe it to yourself to evaluate each candidate that you planned to see. Then make a decision based upon all of the information you've gathered.

DON'T TAPE THE INTERVIEW

Under no circumstances should you tape the candidate *with* or *without* permission. To do so *without* permission is an invasion of privacy. To do so *with* permission does little to help build rapport between you and the prospect. Keep in mind that one of your objectives is to make the candidate feel comfortable. It would be difficult for anyone to relax if they knew they were being taped or filmed.

In addition, increasingly popular video-conference interviewing can be unnerving for even the most self-assured candidates. Forego your urge to record; instead do a good job of interviewing and make notes when you're finished to help jog your memory later.

TAKING NOTES CAN INTERFERE WITH CONCENTRATION

Interviewers that take notes during the interview risk breaking eye contact and losing rapport. When this happens you also risk losing the candidate to someone that gives the candidate his or her full attention and thus appears to be totally interested in the conversation. Competition is fierce for qualified people. Anything you can do to eliminate doubt in the mind of the candidate is worth doing. If you take notes during the interview, you may create a barrier between you and the people you want to hire.

ASK PERMISSION TO TAKE NOTES

Start by saying:

> *"Do you mind if I take notes? I want to be sure that I understand and remember what you're telling me."*

If the candidate tells you he or she would prefer that you not take notes respect that request and write your notes after the interview.

However, be aware that what you write on a résumé and/or application could get you into trouble if it's not job-related. Should those documents be subpoenaed to a court of law, you'll be asked to defend your comments. There's no place for words such as "seems sharp for a blonde," "talks with a lisp," "great body," or anything that's not related to whether or not the candidate can perform the job for which he or she was interviewed.

COMPLETE YOUR NOTES IN MORE DETAIL

If you decide to take notes during the interview, keep your notes to a minimum, just enough to remind yourself of what was said. After the interview, fill in the details with the facts. Recording subjective "impressions" can be dangerous as stated in the previous point. Some hiring managers like to record notes during or after the interview on a "separate" piece of paper. This strategy can be equally as dangerous.

> *For example:* To write on an application that the applicant said that he was recently released from prison is a fact that can be recorded. However, to embellish your comment by saying: "There's no way I'd take a chance and hire a no-good bum like that," could get you into trouble should the applicant later challenge you because he or she didn't get the job.

SCHEDULE BREAKS

Some hiring managers schedule too many interviews in one day. It's not only hard on the managers but also the candidates that may be shuffled from one interviewer to the other. When fatigue sets in, it can be difficult to conduct an accurate evaluation of the candidates. Save a few minutes between each interview to catch your breath and take a few notes if you need to. When you schedule interviews too close together or too many in one day, you risk confusion and may get to the point where you rush through the interview in an effort to get done without regard to whether or not you obtained the information you were looking for. The more thorough, professional, targeted, and legal your interviewing skills, the better the candidate will understand your company, the job requirements, and what it would be like to work for you.

DON'T ALLOW THE "HALO EFFECT" TO INFLUENCE YOUR DECISION

The "halo effect" is about judging a candidate on one good quality without regard to weaknesses or concerns that you may have. For example, you like the fact that the candidate has three years of research and development experience and that strength overshadows a concern you have about the candidate's exceptionally boisterous personality. You value the experience, but the job requires a tactful individual that can balance the challenge of the job with all of the different people he or she will be working with on a regular basis. You let the "halo effect" interfere with your hiring decision.

BE SURE ALL TEAM MEMBERS UNDERSTAND THEIR RESPONSIBILITIES

Team interviewing can be risky business. It can also be an effective way to learn more about candidates. There are two approaches to team interviews. One is sequential whereby candidates are interviewed by several people but one-on-one. The second, less popular approach is a panel interview. Here a candidate sits before a group of people that takes turns asking questions.

Whether you decide on a panel or sequential approach, each interviewer should be assigned specific questions to ask and have answered. Avoiding overlap will prevent the candidate from being bored and possibly annoyed. In addition, this technique is a great way to get maximum use of the interviewers' time. Once you complete all the interviews, compare candidates against one another and make a team decision about which candidate(s) best meets your job requirements.

BE PREPARED FOR CANDIDATES' QUESTIONS

Most candidates will have questions to ask you. Well-prepared candidates may even have a list of items they wish to have answered before accepting your job offer.

Questions generally fall into the following two categories:

- **Job-oriented**—shows an interest in the details of the job, and growth opportunities.

- **Self-oriented**—covers compensation and benefits, interaction with others and questions related to "what's in it for me?"

One of your jobs as the hiring manager is to be prepared to answer the candidates' questions. Most candidates are interested in knowing more about the job as well as the opportunities for learning and promotion. You can be sure that questions on these subjects will come up; you need to be able to truthfully answer job-oriented questions if you hope to attract and keep good people.

Questions related to compensation and benefits along with *"what's in it for me"* questions, will come up most often at the end of the interview. Many candidates have been coached to not ask about these things until they get the job offer or at the very least until the end of the "final" interview. However, some companies provide a package of information to all candidates at the end of the first interview. Regardless of when the subject comes up, the hiring manager must be fully prepared to answer questions in this area as well.

REVIEW YOUR PERFORMANCE

As you conclude the interview, consider how well you've done. Would you interview differently the next time? Did you ask questions that helped you make a good decision either before or against the candidate? Were the questions you asked within your rights to ask or did you seek information about race, color, creed, age, and national origin or handicap status? If you did, you violated the law and ran the risk of being caught and challenged. Keep interviews friendly, but at a professional level. Candidates are judging you just as you are evaluating them.

> *In summary: The interview is the most important part of the hiring process. You have much to gain by taking to heart the ideas shared in this chapter. Keep in mind, however, that interviewing is a learned skill and it takes practice. Unless you're a human resource professional that hires people for a*

living, chances are you may feel like you could use more practice in this area.

Without a good system for interviewing, you take a chance in selecting candidates who may fail. Losses of one-half to ten times an individual's yearly salary are typical when the wrong person is chosen for a position. Can you afford to take that kind of risk? Is your budget ready for an unnecessary drain of profits because of poor selection decisions?

After you've studied the ideas presented here, take time to think about what you did well and what you could do better the next time. Keep working to improve and you soon will be hiring based on skills and experience rather than on intuition or gut feelings, as many inexperienced hiring managers do.

THERE'S NO MAGIC BULLET

(pre-employment testing)

THIS CHAPTER IS ABOUT TESTING. Some managers "shoot themselves in the foot" when they decide to test applicants before they hire. Many unsuspecting managers have found themselves in trouble because they tested people without regard to the legitimacy of the test instrument. Should you decide to test, you'll want to be sure you're familiar with state and local municipal laws as well as federal discrimination, privacy and negligence laws.

Even companies that are ultimately successful in defending illegal or inappropriate testing often find themselves in a costly battle to defend their actions. There's no magic bullet. There are no guarantees that your decision to test won't be challenged by a candidate that doesn't get the job.

It's not sufficient to show a lack of discriminatory intent if the selection instrument discriminates against one group more than another. Second, the burden of proof falls upon the employer to show that employment requirements are directly job-related.

There are situations when managers or groups of employees without regard or understanding as to whether or not the tests are job-related develop pre-employment tests. In some cases, they have little to do with the skills required of the future employee and are thus a liability. Several things to consider when deciding to test include where are you going to get the test, who will administer the test, and to whom will it be administered?

If you decide to use a pre-employment test you'll find that they're typically grouped into the following categories:

- Written tests concerning job knowledge.

- Personality tests including the testing of honesty, integrity, behavioral characteristics, and leadership style.

- Performance tests of job skills and abilities.

- Interpersonal tests (a job interview, role-play, group exercises).

- Medical evaluation.

- Reference checks prior to employment.

- Investigative reports including credit check and driving record.

Professionally developed tests will get more accurate results and offer a higher probability of hiring quality personnel. You can buy the tests you need from a reputable company such as Psychological Corporation in San Antonio, Texas (1-800-211-8378).

TESTS MUST NOT DISCRIMINATE AGAINST ANY PROTECTED GROUP

To avoid liability, you must be able to show that:

- Test questions don't screen out a disproportionately large number of minorities.

- All tests are directly related to the specific position that you're trying to fill. You may be asked to prove that there's a direct correlation between what you require of candidates and what's actually needed for success on the job.

- The level of difficulty of pre-employment tests can't be unreasonable. Unnecessarily high standards often exclude qualified people who don't have a formal education but who can still perform the job.

There are many state and federal laws that govern pre-employment testing along with privacy rights and negligence laws. They also protect the individual's right to equal opportunity without regard to race, color, sex, religion, national origin and physical handicap. Make sure you know the laws before engaging in pre-employment screening of this nature.

DON'T RELY ON PRE-EMPLOYMENT TESTS AS A HIRE/NOT HIRE TOOL

You make a big investment in time, money and energy when you hire. If you were to make a major purchase you would at the least take time to decide what you wanted. If it were a car you probably would want to test-drive several models. Preparing to hire is no different. Pre-employment tests can be a useful tool.

They should be used in conjunction with an interview and a check of references. To make a hire/not hire decision based on test scores is like robbing yourself of the "rest of the story." A positive attitude and willingness to take on new challenges is still important when it comes to hiring a team player that's going to fill the position that you have in mind.

PRE-EMPLOYMENT TESTS SHOULD BE USED AS ADDITIONAL SELECTION INFORMATION

Think of the pre-employment test as supplemental to the interview, just like a reference check. The information gained from the results of the test can be valuable if taken in perspective. Many organizations successfully use professionally developed pre-employment screening devices that fall into the categories of honesty, achievement, personality, psychological, medical, drug, alcohol, and even handwriting analysis which some critics view as an invasion of an individual's right to privacy. Think twice before you administer pre-employment tests and make sure you're purchasing the tests from a credible source.

THE BEST TEST IS A TRIAL WORK PERIOD

If you really want to know what people are like on the job, arrange for a trial work period to last from a few days to several weeks. Another way to get to know future employees is to hire temporary workers and consider the days worked as a way to test or try out individuals that the managers want to consider for regular employment.

This "test" works well for many employers as well as prospective employees who have a chance to decide if the job meets their expectations. Wouldn't you rather find out before someone is on the company payroll that they can't do the job or are not interested enough to do their best?

KNOW THE LAW UNDER ADA
BEFORE TESTING

The American With Disabilities Act (ADA) is modeled after the regulations implementing section 504 of the Rehabilitation Act of 1973, including the requirement for reasonable accommodation and the inclusion of modified examinations as a form of accommodation. Before testing, employers should understand the legal requirements and psychometric issues that must be considered in using selection tests under the ADA.

In brief, there are three types of information that must be considered in using selection tests under the ADA. First, employers must be familiar with the legal requirements of the ADA and the rationale behind these requirements. Second, employers should be aware of the specific role of their tests in helping to select qualified employees (in other words, the validity basis for their tests). Third, employers should be familiar with the types of accommodations that are most likely to be effective in preserving the reliability and validity of the tests for people with various disabilities.

In addition, under the ADA, it is discriminatory to use selection criteria that screen out or tend to screen out individuals with disabilities unless the criteria are shown to be job-related for the position in question and are consistent with business necessity. This is to ensure that tests don't act as barriers to the employment of persons with disabilities unless the person is unable to do the job, even with reasonable accommodation.

Employers should design selection criteria for jobs to ensure a close fit between the selection criteria and an individual's ability to do the job. A criterion that tends to screen out a person with a disability must be shown to be job-related for the position and consistent with business necessity. To be consistent with business necessity a criterion must be related to an essential job function. The obligation to make reasonable accommodation means that an employer must make modifications or adjustments to the application process that would enable a qualified individual with a disability to be considered for the position he or she desires.

RESOURCES:

ADA Regional Disability and Business Technical Assistance Center Hotline (800) 949-4232 (voice/TTY)

Equal Employment Opportunity Commission, 1801 "L" Street, NW, Washington, DC 20507, (800) 669-4000 (Voice) to reach EEOC field offices; for publications call (800) 669-EEOC or (800) 800-3302 (voice/TTY).

> *In summary:* Pre-employment testing can be a valuable tool for evaluating future employees. It can be affordable, easy to use and administer and customizable so that you're checking for what's important to you.
>
> *Some of the qualities you may wish to test are:*
>
> • *Ability to control emotions*
>
> • *Ability to influence others*
>
> • *Assertiveness*
>
> • *Attention to detail*

- *Attitude towards customer service*

- *Attitude towards supervision*

- *Dependability*

- *Energy*

- *Honesty*

- *Illegal drug avoidance*

- *Values*

- *Willingness to take calculated risks*

In Summary: *Whether you choose an on-the-job trial test or a traditional pencil and paper general aptitude test, you'll want to be sure that your tests are unbiased. This can be tricky. Consult with a psychologist or qualified test specialist before you proceed.*

If you chose to test for alcohol and illegal drugs, you'll also be governed by a set of rules that dictate when and how these tests can be administered to prospective employees. Proceed with caution and you will most likely be pleased with the results of your decision to test.

Remember, if you utilize testing you have to do it in a non-discriminatory fashion. In other words, everyone who meets the criteria for the job and who is being considered for the position needs to be given this test—not just minorities or someone who "looks like" a questionable candidate.

THE FITNESS REPORT

(the value of references)

RESEARCH INDICATES that almost 25% of all résumés include misleading information or outright lies. The most common form of deception involves overstating education followed by inflation of job responsibilities. Checking references can sometimes reveal these deceits. You may be thinking, "Why bother to check references? Employers won't tell me anything because they're afraid of being sued." That's not necessarily the case if you ask only job-related questions. Use a direct approach. Keep the questions strictly focused on learning more about performance, skill level and specific job training. Once the reference feels comfortable with you, information will be easier to attain.

You'll do two things when you check references—verify the facts and solicit opinions. The most effective way to validate background information is to use preprinted forms with fill-in-the-blank statements for verifying education, former place of employment, etc. Include a section that authorizes the release of information and have the applicant sign it. You may want to check with your legal department for wording. Then follow up with each reference by telephone if you don't get your answers within a reasonable amount of time. Many employers skip the fill-in-the-blank form and go straight to the phone. Use a list of questions to guide your phone discussion. Take appropriate notes, particularly if you have references to check on many applicants. Modern militaries have a variety of methods for gathering intelligence. One source is old-fashioned human intelligence. Businesses do it everyday in gathering marketing data as well as checking references on job applicants.

As mentioned in Chapter 3, employment applications are important. A résumé is not an application. Request that at the very least your final candidates complete an application containing authorization to allow former employers to release information. The authorization should clearly state that the applicant agrees to hold those that provide the references harmless in the event the applicant is denied employment as a result of an unfavorable reference.

Many state laws were written to protect employers who in good faith tell the truth as they see it. However, it's still a good idea to ask employees to sign a release stating that you, as their former employer, have permission to speak with their references.

Ideally, you'll want to check references yourself. You may have someone in the human resources department do the work for you, but you run the risk that the reference checker won't be as familiar with the job requirements as you are. This can lead to a less than satisfactory outcome. Some businesses hire a reference checking service. If you decide to hire such a service, be sure you feel totally comfortable with the quality of their work. You may have to check their references to get this information.

Finally, you can't ask the references anything that the law doesn't permit you to ask the applicant. That includes questions regarding age, religion, race, marital status, children or child care arrangements, parents, residence, health status, psychological well-being, financial obligations, previous arrests, memberships in social organizations, or visible characteristics.

DEVELOP RAPPORT

- Identify yourself, your organization and your reason for calling. Assure them that all information will remain confidential.

- Approach references with respect for their time. If the reference hesitates to speak with you, offer to leave your name and a phone number where they may call you back (a way to verify you are who you say you are).

- Verify the information provided by the candidate using "closed" questions. A "closed" question is one to which only a "yes" or "no" can be answered. For example, you might ask: "Was the candidate employed with you from January 1998 until September 2000?" The reference will answer "yes" or "no." Ask "closed" questions to break the ice and ease into the conversation.

As soon as you feel the reference is willing to volunteer information, shift to "open" questions. "Open" questions start with one of the following words: "Who," "What," "When," "Where," "Why," and "How." For example, you might ask: "How does this person typically react under pressure?" or "What is his or her biggest strength (or weakness)?" Ask "open" questions to get the reference talking. Just be careful that your questioning doesn't become an inquisition.

MOST REFERENCES WILL VERIFY THE FACTS

There's a lot of talk about references being reluctant to give information, and many are. However, most references will verify the facts. At the very least you should be able to get what you need regarding dates employed, job title, and possibly even verification of salary information. Listen for enthusiasm in answers to your questions. There's a big difference between: "Yes, she worked here" and "we really hated to see her go!"

SPEAK WITH WORK-RELATED REFERENCES ONLY

Some hiring managers ask for personal references. A doctor, minister, rabbi, or neighbor can't offer the same insight into the candidate's work performance that a former supervisor or manager can. Make the best use of your time by speaking only with those who can supply you with the information you need. If the candidate volunteered time to a special cause or charity, a reference from a supervisor could also be valuable.

Written letters of reference are also of little value. At the very least you can expect to read a neutral report from a supervisor. No one in his right mind would write a poor reference and hand it to an employee to show to prospective employers. An applicant's personal friend, neighbor, doctor, etc. may write a glowing recommendation but knows nothing about that individual's work performance.

ASK THE SAME OR SIMILAR QUESTIONS OF EACH REFERENCE

The best way to compare one candidate against another when checking references is to ask the same or similar questions about each candidate when you speak to their references. Prepare your questions, just as you would for the interview. Know what you need to know and be prepared to probe for addtional information if you are not satisfied with what you hear.

For example, you might ask the following "open" questions:

- Can you give me an example of a time when the candidate was asked to work on an assignment outside of his or her regular job responsibilities?

- What kinds of people does he or she get along with best?

- Tell me about a time when there was a communication breakdown between you and the individual we're discussing.

- What kind of career progress do you feel this person made while working for you?

- How many hours on average did he or she work each week?

- Give me an example of a time when you as the manager placed excessive demands on the candidate.

- What were his or her three most impressive contributions to your company?

BE CAREFUL WHAT YOU ASK

Many managers seem to be confused about what they can and cannot ask references. Some believe what's legally unacceptable to ask the candidate can be explored with the reference. This is incorrect and could lead to serious problems. You can't ask anything of the reference that you can't lawfully ask the candidates themselves. For example, you can't ask the candidate about marital status or number of children. You can't ask the reference either. It's pretty simple. Ask only job-related questions. If you're in doubt, don't ask.

SPEAK WITH A CANDIDATE'S PEER OR DIRECT REPORT

A peer or direct-report can be an excellent resource for the person checking the references. These people work closely with the candidate and should be able to provide you with valuable information. Sometimes when candidates are asked for three references, they'll ask if one can be a peer or direct report. Ask the same good questions of these people and you can add to your opinions about the candidate.

YOU COULD BE HELD LIABLE FOR HIRING PEOPLE WHO LATER COMMIT A CRIME

If you don't check references or aren't thorough in your efforts, this exercise can be a waste of time. There are a number of documented cases where people with criminal records were hired and later committed a crime. That alone is reason to do a good job of checking references. You could also be held liable for failing to disclose such activity as bringing a firearm to work or assaulting a fellow employee.

USE REFERENCES AS A CONFIRMATION

What you learn from the references should confirm what you already know based on the job interviews and pre-employment tests. If you find inconsistencies in what references are telling you about a candidate, question further.

> **For example:** *A reference said that a candidate was short-tempered. Another of the candidate's references hadn't seen that side of her. But the third and fourth references confirmed that the individual was known to have "adult temper tantrums" when things didn't work out to her satisfaction. In this case, several answers to questions during the interview suggested that the candidate had problems controlling her emotions on the job. The references confirmed what the interviewer suspected and the woman was not hired for a position as a daycare worker.*

BE PREPARED TO "GIVE" A REFERENCE

The question often arises: "What should I say when I'm asked to give a reference on a former employee?" First, it's important to follow your company policy. Most organizations have a "gatekeeper" policy whereby only specific individuals in the work unit are authorized to provide employment references.

However, if you are authorized to give references, consider the following Do's and Don'ts before speaking:

- *Do* ask for the requester's name, company and telephone number and return their call.

- *Do* give an evaluation of the former employee's job performance, upon request only, to prospective employers.

- *Do* give prospective employers, upon request, information concerning employment verification on the position the employee held.

- *Do* give truthful information to prospective employers whether you view it as positive or negative.

- *Do* have solid documentation to substantiate information given to prospective employers.

- *Do* thoroughly investigate the facts underlying the employee's evaluation prior to making comments to prospective employers.

- *Don't* volunteer job performance evaluations if the prospective employer doesn't specifically request the information.

- *Don't* give information that is knowingly false, deliberately misleading, or rendered with a malicious purpose.

- *Don't* give information without reviewing as many pertinent facts as possible concerning the employee's job performance.

- *Don't* give information without consulting the author, if available, of the employee's evaluation for specific facts. It's generally safer to give out information contained in the official personnel file.

- *Don't* give information that hasn't been documented.

- *Don't* assume all phone inquiries are legitimate.

In summary: *Reference checks are an important part of the hiring process, but one that is often taken lightly or overlooked. There seems to be an attitude of: "References only talk about the candidate's strengths, so why bother to check them?" Not true! If you're committed to gathering accurate information from references, you may be surprised at what you find. Probe for the facts.*

In addition, some employers are reluctant to provide references because they view themselves at risk should the former employee sue them if the reference information they provided was unfavorable and they didn't offer them a job. The claim that former employees are most likely to assert is that the references are false and damaging to their reputation and, therefore, defamatory.

However, be aware that some states offer "qualified immunity" from civil liability for employers who disclose information, whether positive or negative relating to the job performance of former employees to the former employee's prospective employers.

Regardless of the time and effort it takes to check references, it's worth the investment provided you do a thorough job of checking work-related references only. In addition, don't fall into the trap of hearing only what you want to hear. Some hiring managers are so excited about the candidate that they fail to listen with a critical ear; they hear only the good, when in reality, there may be some negatives that should be considered when making the job offer. No one is a "perfect ten."

THE SELECTION BOARD RECOMMENDATION

(making the final hiring decision)

WHEN YOU GET TO THE POINT where you're ready to make a decision and hire, make sure you do so expeditiously. Many good candidates have been lost to the competition because the manager(s) found it difficult to come to a conclusion. Or perhaps, the manager was so busy that he or she procrastinated in favor of completing other tasks. Whatever the reason, it's important to make a decision as quickly as reasonably possible and make a job offer to the best candidate(s).

However, before you extend an offer, you'll want to be sure that you're making the right decision. There are no guarantees that the individual you select will be the right fit, but if you've done your homework, you increase the probability of making the right choice the first time.

This chapter offers tips for making the final selection. It includes a suggestion to use a candidate rating form that can be useful when comparing one candidate against another. It also addresses the issue of "team" interviewing which can be invaluable or a disaster, depending upon your approach and that of your employees.

Take this part of the interview process seriously. Don't be like the manager who said regarding hiring:

"You win some and you lose some."

That may be the case; a certain amount of turnover is inevitable; but you'll want to carefully select and keep as many people as you can. So, be prepared to invest some valuable time and energy in the selection process. The pay-off is worth the effort.

IN MAKING THE FINAL SELECTION, REVIEW:

- **The job description** to remind yourself of what you're looking for. Is the candidate you've chosen for the position someone who can handle the job duties you have listed?

- **The specific job requirements.** You'll want to be sure that you're matching the candidate to the job, not the job requirements to the candidate.

- **Your interview notes.** If you took notes before and/or after the interview, review your notes before making the final decision. There may be something that needs additional probing. Don't hesitate to call a candidate before making the job offer if you have some unanswered questions.

USE A RATING SYSTEM

How do you make the final hiring determination? If you rely exclusively on your "gut feelings," you risk making a bad choice. People aren't always what they appear to be. A rating system helps assure that you won't be impressed with one particular qualification to the exclusion of others. A good system will help you rate candidates against your job requirements. It's often difficult to choose between several qualified people, so having the comparison scores can serve as a valuable tool. Each person who interviews a candidate should complete an interview rating form.

If you're conducting team interviews, you also need a system for collecting data. A rating system will help everyone get an idea of how the candidate was judged by each interviewer. Oftentimes, teams have a difficult time agreeing on hiring decisions. Maybe one teammate saw a different and disturbing side of the candidate and feels making a job offer would be a mistake. Perhaps one team member feels exceptionally positive about the candidate while the rest of the team feels neutral. How do you come to a decision?

HIRE PEOPLE THAT WILL BE COMFORTABLE WITH YOU AND YOUR TEAM

The simple statement, "Hire for attitude; everything else is secondary," is a valuable piece of advice. A highly skilled person with a questionable attitude will most likely create more problems than you're prepared to handle. It's a fact that most people spend more time at work than they do at home. You want to foster an environment that people gravitate toward, not a depressing or angry place where no one wants to work. Hire people that fit the culture of your company and your department. To do anything less could lead to disaster.

NO ONE IS PERFECT

It's easy to get caught up in the frenzy of finding the best candidate in the world, especially for positions that require unique skills. However, the reality is that no one is perfect. Don't make the job requirements and your search unnecessarily difficult.

> *For example: A manager sought a secretary that could type 130 words per minute because of the volume of work he needed done every day. He conducted an exhaustive search to no avail. Looking back on the search, the manager realized that his*

expectations were unrealistic, that he had wasted valuable time in his quest. In another example, a manager wanted the "perfect fit" to fill a vacancy as a marketing manager. After nine months of searching she found someone with the credentials she was seeking, but who lacked an acceptable level of writing skill. The manager decided the ability to write well wasn't as important as the candidate's prior work experience. She hired the candidate after the candidate made a commitment to improve his writing.

In summary: *Good employees, bad employees, employees in general are an endless topic of discussion for many managers. The bottom line is that good employees are a joy and bad employees are a manager's worst nightmare! Why settle for mediocre when you have the option of hiring the best?*

In the words of W. Edwards Deming: "If a person is not performing, it is probably because they have been miscast for the job." Deming also posed this question to Henry Ford: "If your employee is not performing as expected—is it because you hired them that way or made them that way after you hired them?" Deciding whom to hire is an impor-

tant decision, not only for you and your team, but for the individual you plan to make part of your work family. Make sure that you get consensus and hire only those people who exhibit enthusiasm for what you have to offer.

Finally, the question has been asked: "Who's piloting the aircraft?" Is it you and your sense of good judgment or are you being influenced by others in your organization that consciously or unconsciously make hiring decisions based upon immediate reactions and gut feelings? If that's the case, it might be time to become a "squeaky wheel" and grab the attention of others that may be unrealistically searching for the ideal candidate.

TONS OF DIPLOMACY

(job offers and negotiations)

The toughest part of the job interview is when the talk turns to money. Many people feel uncomfortable discussing salary. Nonetheless, you need to get past your feelings of discomfort on this subject. You're the buyer. You should have a salary range in mind. It shouldn't take you long to find out how much the seller is willing to accept. Unless you have only one price to offer, be prepared to bargain when you reach the point of making the job offer.

Most candidates want to get every dollar the company is willing to part with. Why should they wait a year for a $3,000 raise when they could have it right from the beginning? Many job seekers will have researched your company and know what people in the same or similar positions earn either in your company, other companies or sometimes both.

In many cases, candidates have been coached on how to negotiate salary and benefits. They want the prospective employer to make the opening bid. After you present your offer, expect a counter-offer in which the candidate re-emphasizes two or three specific qualifications in which you're especially interested.

Although some companies are not willing to negotiate, most are. If you're a company that doesn't, let candidates know that your first offer is your only offer. In lieu of money, consider negotiating benefits such as a sign-on bonus, extra vacation days, tuition reimbursement, a compressed work week or an earlier than scheduled salary review.

Once you've gone as far as you can with negotiations, don't be surprised if the candidate asks for time to think about it. A reasonable amount of time is several days to a week. If you want the candidate bad enough, you may have to wait longer and/or offer more.

MAKE THE OFFER WITH CONFIDENCE

In making the job offer ask:

> *"What kind of money are you looking for?*
> *What would be the least you'd be willing to*
> *accept?"*

Whether you decide to ask this question as you start the interviewing process or wait until you've identified your finalists, this is a great way to find out what the candidate has in mind. Although you're thinking about a pre-determined amount, you may find that your top pick is expecting to work for more than you can afford to pay. If that's the case, the decision is yours as to whether to offer more.

You're in a great position if your offer seems generous. It's possible that the candidate doesn't know her worth in the labor market and is underselling herself. Candidates that have researched salary levels should have a realistic idea of what employers are willing to pay. But in the event that you do offer more than expected, it could be enough to close the deal with a great candidate.

INCLUDE CONTINGENCIES

If you require a pre-employment test of any kind including a drug screen, your offer should be predicated on the candidate passing the test. Some companies also require a pre-employment physical as a condition of employment. This should also be mentioned with your offer. Some final candidates may be reluctant or even refuse a pre-employment test maybe out of fear or perhaps there's something to conceal. It's better to find this out before you make a commitment to hire just in case there's a problem.

DON'T SUCCUMB TO PRESSURE

Candidates are eager to know what you think about them, but don't let them pressure you into making a decision. Some may have other offers, but would rather work for you. Candidates sometimes will call asking when you're going to make a decision. Don't feel rushed if you're undecided. However, many hiring managers make the mistake of taking too long to make a decision and end up losing the candidate to a competitor. You may not have any control over company politics and the hiring process, but if you have anything to say about the speed in which a job offer is made, you're fortunate. Time is of the essence when it comes to identifying and hiring top talent.

ALLOW ENOUGH TIME FOR A RESPONSE

In your need to hire someone as soon as possible, you may be tempted to put pressure on the candidate to accept your offer immediately or within a day or two. Candidates that you're attracted to are also most likely of interest to your competition. To force a decision before the candidate feels comfortable could be a mistake. Someone that accepts an offer, starts the job, and quickly leaves because he or she is unhappy with a hasty decision to say "yes" may cause problems for everyone.

BE PREPARED TO NEGOTIATE

You make an offer. The candidate hesitates. You wait for a response. The candidate tells you he was looking for

$10,000 more than you're planning to pay. Now what? Don't give up. Although compensation is a big motivator, research indicates that money is not typically the number one deciding factor. The entire "package" including benefits can add a lot of value to your offer. In addition, most people want to work in a pleasant work environment, a place where they feel like part of a team. Challenge and opportunity for growth could be another important selling point. In any event, you need to anticipate negotiations and be ready for them.

CONFIRM THE OFFER IN WRITING

There's no substitute for a written contract. A handshake is nice but not enough to detail what you and the candidate have agreed upon. A simple letter that confirms start date, salary, vacation days, bonus plan and anything else that was discussed and agreed to should be included in your letter.

> *In summary: Negotiations should be expected. In fact, the more sophisticated the candidate and level of the position, the more likely you will receive a counter-offer. Even if your offer is generous, don't be surprised if the prospective new employee hesitates and asks for time to "think about it." You may feel like you need an immediate answer, but don't pressure the candidate if you have any hopes of having your offer accepted. "Never offer more than they ask for" is the advice of many experts on salary negotiations.*

If it's not within your scope of responsibility or authority to negotiate, tell the candidate that you'll get back to him with an answer. Just don't take too long or you run the risk of losing him to the competition. You can be assured that there are plenty of competitors that will be quick to move on a "yes, but" response from prospective employees who want more salary and/or benefits than you initially offered.

Be prepared for candidates who ask for clarification. Some candidates will want more information on health benefits, your 401K plan and vacation. Sharp candidates will be watching for a sign of your willingness to be flexible. Some will use silence to their advantage giving the impression that they are not particularly interested in your offer. They also recognize the fact that timing is everything. If you run into a roadblock, be prepared to compromise; then close the deal.

TRACK THEM ON YOUR RADAR SCREEN

(stay in touch)

T HE WAR FOR TALENT IS REAL. Hiring requires a lot of time and energy with the ultimate goal of making the right decision. Unfortunately, new-hires often get lost in the shuffle because not enough care has been taken to insure they get a good start. Keep in mind that when someone joins your organization they've left behind their support system and all that's familiar to them. Most likely they'll join you with a bit of apprehension concerning what it will be like to work for you.

Undesired attrition is expensive. How do you plan to keep the people you've worked so hard to find and hire? In addition, all new hires, whether internal or external, go through three stages:

- *The anticipation stage*—the new hire has given notice and is waiting to join your team. He or she is wondering what it will be like to work for you. It means leaving behind things that are familiar like friends, office space, a good (or bad) supervisor and even the familiar way in which he or she drove to work.

- *The reality stage*—It's beginning to seem real. They've left the past behind and started working for you. Are you ready for them? Will you be there the day they start work or will someone else represent you and help them get acquainted?

- *The judgment stage*—The new hire is making a decision at this time as to whether or not to stick around. If you're going to lose him, research shows that most turnover takes place during the first 90 days on the job. Part of your responsibility as a hiring manager is to make sure he's happy because if he isn't, he's history and you'll have to start your candidate search over again unless you're prepared to offer the job to your second choice.

DON'T ASSUME ANYTHING

After you've made the job offer you'll probably move onto other things and wait for the new employee to start work.

However, if you don't have a plan to stay in contact with the person you offered the job to, you risk losing him to someone else. Many candidates will give "notice" to their current employer. That could mean one or more weeks before they join your organization. Stay in touch by telephone. Invite the person for lunch or dinner. Or consider sending a fruit basket to the new employee as a way to say "welcome." Don't assume that just because your offer has been accepted that you've got a new member for your team.

SEND A PERSONALIZED NOTE

Immediately upon acceptance of your job offer send a note or card that's personally signed by everyone in the department welcoming the new-hire to the company. For example, a woman accepted a job offer and soon received a note signed by everyone on the team she was about to join. "I knew then I had made the right decision," said the woman. She kept the card on her desk while she worked out her notice. The day she arrived there was another card waiting for her that was personally signed by her new teammates. Everyone joined in the celebration of her arrival with a potluck lunch.

ROLE-OUT THE WELCOME MAT

On the day the new hires join your organization, have their business cards waiting for them. It's a great way to say: "welcome." What about their office or workspace? Is the software loaded on the computer? Do they have the supplies they'll need? Who will show them the restrooms, break room or cafeteria as well as other important areas of the company? The better prepared you are for their arrival, the smoother the transition you can expect on the part of the new employee into your culture and workplace.

PROVIDE NEW HIRE ORIENTATION

There appears to be a direct correlation between retention and orientation to the business. Some organizations have elaborate programs that last for months. Others are shallow; managers spend a few hours with new employees reviewing benefits and the employee handbook. They expect the new hire to get to work without regard to the transitional process ahead.

Whether the new hire is an internal or external candidate, the time during which employees transition is critical to retention. This is the time to help employees explore how they'll make meaningful contributions to the company. You'll want to involve other employees in the orientation process in addition to self-guided learning. The orientation should ideally span the employee's first year of employment, not just a few days or weeks. This is your opportunity to share a comprehensive picture of the company. It's your chance to set the stage for what's ahead.

This is also the time for new employees to begin to make friends. People are less likely to leave a work environment where they feel accepted and have friends. Think of orientation as a process, not a program. It can be a time of difficult transition. It's your job as a manager to make the transition as smooth as possible.

CONSIDER A MENTOR PROGRAM

Do your new hires have a volunteer mentor that can help them learn the routine by answering questions and simply being a friend? In scouting it was called a "buddy." Regardless of the term you use, you'll want to make sure that new hires get off on the right foot. What better way to make people feel welcome than to surround them by people who want them to be happy and successful in their new work environment.

Keep in mind that mentoring cannot be ordered, forced or taught. It's a natural result of harmonious rapport inherent in the people themselves and the relationship they develop. Companies can jump-start mentoring programs by encouraging employees to help others gain a long-term perspective on their skills and how they can lead to a successful career. Offering acceptance and encouragement, increasing self-esteem and assisting the new employees in establishing professional networks are some outcomes of a successful mentoring relationship.

CONSIDER WORK-LIFE PROGRAMS

To increase the chance that new employees will stick with them, many companies are opening child-care centers, permitting job-sharing and part-time employment as well as encouraging telecommuting. They're catering to employees in an effort to keep them on the payroll.

> *For example: A company in Silicon Valley felt it needed to catch up with corporate*

culture elsewhere and move beyond minor perks like concierge services and free coffee and donuts each morning. They now pay for laptops and subsidize second desktop PCs so employees can work from home. They also opened a $10 million dollar child-care center with Web cams so parents can check in on their children.

In summary: *You've worked hard to recruit and hire the best people for the job. You're excited about your decision and eagerly await the arrival of the new employees. If you have any hopes of retaining the new hires, keep them on your radar screen. Stay in contact with them until they start working for you. Then be sure they get all of the encouragement and support they need to stay challenged and motivated to do a good job.*

Take time to meet with them on a regular basis. Communication breakdowns have lead to many terminations and employees walking off the job. Make sure they're adjusting to the change of a new environment. Most people don't relish change, especially if they weren't unhappy in their last job assignment. It's possible they wanted to try something more challenging and were willing to take a risk. They may have the chance to return to a former employer if they're not happy working for you.

Employee retention is one of the most difficult jobs a manager has. Some take it seriously while others neglect their responsibilities in this area. You may be successful in retaining your staff but what about the managers and supervisors who work for you? Are they as competent or do you see them verbally abusing their employees? If you tolerate such actions, you are as much at fault.

Some companies even base performance increases for their managers on the amount of turnover in their departments. The philosophy is that along with other responsibilities, managers and supervisors are accountable for the retention of their staff. It's not a bad way to promote positive relations as well as reduce unnecessary turnover.

APPENDIX

A S YOU PREPARE TO CONDUCT a job interview keep in mind that you'll want to ask questions both to acquire specific information and to assess how the applicant handles the questions. Sometimes you'll gain unexpected insights into an individual's personality or work ethic through a chance remark. You can gather the basic information by simply reading the application or résumé. The interview questions are your opportunity to explore in more detail those things that are important to you including interpersonal skills.

Before you begin an interview, decide which questions you want to ask. While you may explore certain areas such as experience and training for any position within the company, you may want to tailor other questions to meet specific needs.

The following sample questions and what to consider in evaluating responses are categorized for ease of use.

APPLICANTS WHO RESIGNED FROM PREVIOUS JOBS OR WERE TERMINATED

Have you ever been asked to resign from a position? If so, tell me about it.

If an applicant was in a "resign or be fired" situation and chose to resign, he may choose to answer this question with a "no" since in essence he was not asked to resign but given the option of resigning. If you suspect this is the case, you'll want to use additional questions to find out more about the circumstances that prompted the applicant's departure from the previous job.

If an applicant chooses to answer "yes" to this question:

- Does the applicant follow the response with an explanation that appears reasonable and honest or one that seems evasive?

- Does the applicant list the former employer as a reference? To do so could be an indication that the applicant resigned, by suggestion or request, for acceptable reasons.

   Consider this: *A "yes" answer is not necessarily a negative answer. Be sure you get the complete story. People are asked to resign for a variety of reasons. It's not always the* *employee's fault. When an employee fails, the manager needs to accept a share of the responsibility. Oftentimes, there's a breakdown in communication behind a resignation. A minimum of two people are usually involved when someone leaves.*

What do you hope to find or experience in this position that you didn't have in your previous job?

The applicant's answer, in addition to demonstrating whether he or she researched the company before the interview, should also reflect a positive attitude and a desire for continued professional growth. The emphasis in the reply should be on the positive aspects of the hoped-for new position rather than the negative aspects of the previous situation.

> *Consider this: A flippant answer alerts you to an attitude that may have contributed to the applicant's problems with another employer. Are you willing to risk that same kind of attitude once the applicant becomes an employee of your organization? "Sour grapes" often reflects more on the applicant than on his or her past employment situation.*

What do you feel you learned from your previous job that you could apply to future employment?

You can ask this question of all applicants who have prior work experience, but you have an additional reason to ask applicants who resigned or were terminated for reasons other than downsizing, layoffs, and company closings. Answers can reveal whether they gained insight concerning difficulties at the former job and understand how to now apply that hard-gained wisdom to a new situation.

> *Consider this: Everyone makes mistakes. Some learn from their mistakes, some don't. Find people who learn quickly and are ready to move on and grow with your business.*

Your application lists many job changes. Tell me about that.

Experienced interviewers usually view frequent job changes as a "red flag warning." This question gives such applicants a chance to explain/justify their job history. Interviewees shouldn't be surprised at this type of question. In addition to evaluating their explanations of the job history, watch for visible signs of discomfort, attempts to gloss over questionable situations and vague answers.

> *Consider this: Even if the applicant's job history indicates a pattern of job change as a ladder for professional growth, are you willing to be one more rung on that ladder?*

Maybe you're willing to accept someone that may only want to work for you for a brief time before moving on.

Have you thought about leaving your present position before now? If yes, what held you back?

Reasons for such decisions may include financial considerations, a decision to acquire additional education before making a change, pressure by a manager to stay, or personal and family considerations. Unfortunately, such elements as indecisiveness, lack of initiative, and fear of failure may also be part of these decisions. Your goal is to determine what the explanation reveals about the applicant and also whether the reason given is acceptable to you as a prospective employer.

> **Consider this:** *Knowing what holds people back is as important as knowing what causes them to move forward. Some people hold onto a job because they are too lazy to look for another. They're often miserable and tend to create morale problems among their co-workers. These are the people you'll want to avoid hiring.*

Have you ever been passed over for a promotion? If so, tell me about it.

Someone who's not considered for a promotion may resign or decide to seek a new job as a way to handle the anger and disappointment. If unfairly passed over, the person may have made a good decision provided he or she handles it professionally.

Explore with applicants who answer "yes" to this question exactly why they felt they were qualified for the promotion and why they believe they didn't get the job for which they applied. Listen for indications of personal bias, lack of understanding, and poor judgment. Also listen for reasonable and convincing explanations.

> **Consider this:** *Life isn't always fair. In many cases, neither is the manner in which people are promoted. There are times in everyone's life when we don't get what we feel we deserve. How we handle that disappointment is often the difference between success and mediocrity.*

WORK EXPERIENCE AND QUALIFICATIONS

Tell me about the part-time and temporary jobs you've listed on your application.

This is an open question and one you're likely to ask someone entering the labor market after graduation from high school or college. However, you may also decide to ask this question of someone seeking full time, permanent employment that worked at part-time or temporary jobs after leaving another position.

This question provides applicants who are recent graduates with an opportunity to highlight their initiative, work
ethics, experience gained and the usefulness of that experience, and newly acquired skills. Explore how applicants feel
about the job(s) and their attitude towards jobs that served
little purpose other than to provide income.

For applicants who worked part-time and temporary jobs
after leaving a full time, permanent job, this provides an
opportunity for them to present themselves in the best possible light.

> *Consider this: An applicant who was willing
> to work hard at a part-time or temporary job
> to provide income while seeking employment
> in his or her field of work often has a good
> work ethic.*

What experience did you gain from previous jobs that you feel you could apply to this job?

With this question, you're looking for both general and specific areas of experience. You also want applicants to tell
you their understanding of how they can use that experience
in the position for which they've applied.

> *Consider this: Applicants who don't under-
> stand how to use their experience, or can't
> convince you that the previous experience
> served some useful purpose other than pro-
> viding a paycheck, may not have a good*

understanding of their own qualifications or lack of, for the job.

Tell me about your biggest accomplishments

The applicant's answer to this question should preferably deal with an example that relates in some way to the demands of the position for which he or she is interviewing. A major accomplishment, if it doesn't relate to the job in question, should at least demonstrate a highly desirable attribute.

An applicant who has thoroughly prepared for the interview will usually have anticipated this question and be able to answer it easily and with confidence. Unprepared candidates may have difficulty answering you.

> **Consider this:** *If you sense a candidate may be exaggerating, follow up with additional questions. Some interviewees may use a question like this to try to convince you they have more to offer than they actually do.*

To what do you attribute your success in your previous jobs?

Applicants' answers should provide key information concerning what type of person they are, how they approach their work, their work ethic, level of determination, how they handle problems, etc.

> *Consider this: An answer that is intelligent and portrays self-confidence is ideal. A cocky, overly confident answer may serve as a warning that the interviewee could be a problem to manage. No one likes a braggart.*

Describe your activities during a typical day on your last or current job.

Interviewees may choose to give general answers or break the day into time segments. Observe whether an applicant seems comfortable in relating this information, or hesitates. Watch for inconsistencies between information on the résumé or application and verbal answers. Also notice whether the activities described agree with the skills and experience claimed by the applicant.

> *Consider this: If the description of a typical day varies widely from the applicant's description of duties and responsibilities, probe further. It's possible you're looking at a document that stretches the truth. Inflated job responsibilities can be discovered during the interview with a thorough questioning. Just be sure it doesn't become an inquisition.*

Why do you feel you're qualified for this job?

Information on an applicant's résumé or application must have met at least the minimum requirements and qualifications during the initial review of résumés for the applicant to get an interview. Use this question to find out what the candidate can bring to the job that is above and beyond the basic needs of the position.

> ***Consider this:*** *Qualifications may be those of experience, training, a specific skill, or a combination of any of these. Listen carefully for those things that are important to success in the job for which you're interviewing.*

Tell me in as much detail as you can how you would (procedure or method common to the position).

If the position requires knowledge and experience in specific procedures, and if the candidate claims to have that knowledge and experience, he or she should be able to provide this information step-by-step.

> ***Consider this:*** *Anyone can claim to know how to do something and possibly even present a general performance outline. Only someone with actual experience will be able to explain it in detail to your satisfaction.*

What skill did you learn in a previous job that you believe you could use here?

An earlier question concerned experience gained in previous job(s). This question provides applicants with an opportunity to mention specific skills they acquired that enhance their qualifications for the new position. Again, as in other questions, their answers can demonstrate their degree of understanding concerning the requirements of the job.

> **Consider this:** *Some skill levels are easier to determine than others. If necessary and appropriate, you may include a test for skills as part of the interview process. Just be sure you know the proper way to go about this before starting. (See Chapter 6 before implementing any type of pre-employment testing).*

In what ways have your previous jobs prepared you to take on greater responsibilities?

Part of professional growth includes learning how to handle increasingly progressive responsibility. If applicants can't identify ways past jobs did this, they may have avoided responsibility in previous jobs and/or shunned opportunities to learn. Such applicants may not be ready to handle the requirements of a position with greater demands.

> **Consider this:** *People can have good skills. People can have great experience. Neither one guarantee they're ready to take on more responsibility. Attitude is everything!*

ATTITUDE AND INITIATIVE

Tell me about your present/last job.

You can learn a number of things about people from answers to this question. One applicant may give you a well-prepared, thorough and definitive description of his or her present responsibilities. Another may ask for more specifics before answering. Still another may give you a blank stare as he or she struggles to decide how to respond.

If an answer is too lengthy, you may still want to ask some additional questions to determine why the applicant felt a need to "oversell" in the response.

> **Consider this:** *Applicants, who have prepared for the interview by anticipating possible questions, should be able to answer this without too much trouble. It's a great question with which to begin the job interview.*

What did you tell your employer about the need to take time off for this interview?

This question conducts a simple honesty test. Most employees are entitled to some form of time-off (personal days, vacation days, compensatory time), which they can utilize for an interview. Unless the applicant works in a very unusual situation, time off in most cases, shouldn't present a problem.

Consider this: Be aware of the applicant who told a lie to his or her employer. While many people may consider telling an employer they're "going to the doctor" as simply a little white lie, it's still a reason for concern. If they lie to their current employer, someday they'll be lying to you.

How do you feel your present employer treats you?

Even if applicants feel their present employer treats them badly, it reflects poorly on them if they voice their opinion in the interview. An intelligent and reasonable applicant should be able to provide a satisfactory answer to this question without yielding to the temptation to tell you just how terrible their employer treats him or her.

If applicants feel their current employer treats them well, but that they need to seek other employment for reasons such as professional growth, need to relocate, etc., they should provide a brief, simple statement that you as the interviewer may or may not choose to probe further.

Consider this: The overly enthusiastic applicant may be as much of a concern as the applicant who is naive enough to complain to you about his employer.

Tell me about yourself.

Answers to this question can be eye-openers. Experienced candidates should understand that you're asking for a brief, two minute, statement about their interests, skills, education, and past work history. Or, they should ask you for clarification to your question. Inexperienced interviewees may actually start off with where they were born.

> **Consider this:** *Be concerned about the candidate who comes across as deliberately giving you a vague answer. The candidate with a good record wants to use this opportunity to present that record. Ambiguous answers may indicate an attempt on the candidate's part to avoid certain areas of his or her past.*

Why do you want to work for our company?
Why this particular job?

You ask these questions to see whether the applicant took time to research your company and/or the position. The goal is to determine whether the applicant is truly interested in the job and in the company or applied for the job either out of desperation or because the pay seemed attractive.

> **Consider this:** *How can applicants who know nothing at all about your company, its products, its potential, its goal, have a true understanding of whether/how/where they would fit into the company? In addition, the lack of*

preparation may be an indicator of how they approach work responsibilities.

What would you consider to be an ideal work environment?

The response you look for with this question is one that emphasizes the positives: teamwork, common goals, high quality products or services, a certain amount of autonomy, opportunity for advancement and a chance to learn new things. You may, however, receive some surprising answers to this seemingly innocent question.

> **Consider this:** *If the applicant's ideal work atmosphere is contrary to the one that exists in your company, think twice about hiring.*

Do you enjoy a challenge? How do you handle challenges?

Most applicants will automatically respond in the affirmative to the first part of this question, so it's the second part of the question that provides the real insight into the employee's attitude and willingness to confront a challenge. The applicant needs to convince you that he or she will take the initiative when they face a challenge and not wait for someone else to lead the way to a solution.

> **Consider this:** *Most jobs, even the more routine, mundane ones, will involve an occasional challenge. An applicant who is pre-*

pared for the interview will have a good response to this question.

Under what circumstances are you willing to take risks?

Applicants may request more information before responding to this question. Have a specific situation in mind when they ask. You're looking for someone who will not refuse to take a risk if necessary, but will not create a problem by taking unnecessary risks.

> **Consider this:** *Any answer should include awareness of the need to avoid risking reputations—one's personal, other employees', or the company's.*

Tell me about a time when you had to use your initiative.

This question gives the applicant an opportunity to convince you that he or she is someone who gets things done, thereby making life easier for others in the department. An individual who can't provide such an example may be weak in this area.

> **Consider this:** *Even employees whose strong point is that they're good "followers" need to be willing to demonstrate some degree of initiative when the occasion arises.*

How would you prepare to start a major project?

An employee must be able not only to understand the overall picture and the final goal, but also be able to define a good starting point before he or she can successfully complete a project. Look for answers that demonstrate initiative to get the information needed and take the first step toward the goal.

> ***Consider this:*** *Some people tackle a project by doing bits and pieces that demand attention at the moment, with the hope that it will all come together in the end. If the applicant doesn't understand where to start, he or she may have trouble reaching the finish line.*

Do you prefer to set your own goals or work toward pre-determined goals?

Goal-oriented people are usually people with high levels of initiative. Such employees accomplish a great deal. An employee who is content to have only goals pre-determined by others without setting personal goals may meet what is required of them, but may not go the extra mile.

> ***Consider this:*** *As important as it is to set goals, an applicant who comes across as a person who would set unrealistic goals may be as much of a problem as the applicant who appears uninterested in setting any goals.*

SKILLS IN PROBLEM-SOLVING, LEADERSHIP, DECISION-MAKING AND CONFLICT MANAGEMENT

How do you go about solving a problem?
Solving problems involves the following basic steps:

- Identify the problem(s).

- Prepare a plan of action.

- Monitor the progress of that plan.

- Make adjustments if needed to resolve the problem.

Ask for details if you feel an applicant is someone who uses the "putting out fires" approach to problem-solving as many people do.

> ***Consider this:*** *Applicants need to show they understand that before you can solve a problem, you first need to identify its source. If they don't recognize that, they may have trouble solving problems and doing the things you most need done.*

Tell me about the most unusual problem you solved in the past.
This question gives applicants an opportunity to tell you about their ability to tackle and solve out-of-the-ordinary problems, which likely required some unconventional

strategies on their part. The examples can also serve as an indicator of the level of problems they handled. An applicant's example of an unusual problem may even be one you consider an everyday problem that doesn't require much skill to handle.

> ***Consider this:*** *Applicants who respond that they haven't had to solve any unusual problems may be people who handle problems so well they don't consider any problem that unusual. Or they might be the type of person that doesn't recognize problems when they're occurring.*

How do you encourage others to work with you to solve a problem?

Some applicants may indicate they prefer to solve problems alone. If teamwork is important for the position, this could be a concern. Important here, however, is an applicant's ability to both work alone when appropriate, to work with others when appropriate/necessary, and to know which situation he or she faces.

> ***Consider this:*** *If the problem requires assistance from others, does the candidate come across as someone who enlists the help of others, or someone who simply orders others to help?*

Tell me about a specific time when you eliminated or avoided a potential problem before it happened.

In addition to exploring an individual's problem-solving skills, you can gain insight into their degree of initiative and their loyalty to the department and the company. Employees with bad attitudes sometimes adopt a "so what" attitude toward potential problems and allow them to develop into full-blown disasters.

> **Consider this:** *The response doesn't have to involve the elimination of a major problem. It should, however, demonstrate that the applicant possesses the intelligence and ability to identify potential problems and the willingness and initiative to address them before a crisis develops.*

How do you decide what to delegate and to whom?

This question is one you would use primarily when interviewing for management positions. It's important not only to discover how someone delegates, but also to determine whether applicants are willing to delegate. Successful leaders understand the importance of delegating. It benefits both employees who grow through handling additional responsibility and also the manager who has more time for other matters. Applicants who indicate they prefer to do everything themselves may have trouble relinquishing control of even minor details to the people who work for them.

> *Consider this:* A manager's time is too valuable to spend on tasks easily handled by non-management employees. Applicants, who don't understand this basic principle, could be a liability.

How would you describe yourself as a leader? Do you feel you're a natural-born leader?

Some managers lead; some encourage; some dictate; some work beside their employees. Look for applicants who have the right combination of "lead, encourage, and work beside" to get the job done.

Understand what you, the interviewer, consider a "natural born leader" before you ask this question. Otherwise, you may incorrectly evaluate responses from applicants.

> *Consider this:* People may have natural leadership abilities but still need training and experience in using those abilities. Are you prepared to provide the necessary education and training they may need?

What do you consider necessary qualities to be an effective leader?

Now that you've had the applicant tell you how he leads, you can measure that against what he considers leadership qualities. The two answers should support each other.

> ***Consider this:*** *If an applicant describes his or her leadership style one way, but then contradicts that information with the answer to this question, explore further. He or she may be concealing their true leadership style in order to tell you what they think you want to hear.*

What do you think could potentially interfere with your effectiveness as a leader?

Even though applicants may feel that nothing could possibly interfere with their effectiveness, most will not be so egotistical as to state that to the interviewer. However, a number of applicants with absolute confidence in themselves may choose to respond this way.

Some people will choose to acknowledge such a potential but wisely identify something of a minor nature and immediately offer a positive approach to overcoming whatever they name. The interviewer must assess the validity and quality of both types of answers.

> ***Consider this:*** *Be aware that an interviewer's reaction to either of these answers will depend in part upon what he or she seeks in an applicant.*

Would you classify yourself as a quick decision-maker?
If so, why?

Not every decision requires a month of meditation. Not every quick decision is the right one. Applicants need to convince you that while they have the ability to make quick decisions when necessary, they also know that some decisions require time and that they understand the difference.

> **Consider this:** *The best applicant may be the one who feels the best way to serve the interests of the company is to fight for the time necessary to make an important decision.*

What factors do you consider in making a decision?

Effective decision-makers should be able to answer this easily based upon their past experience. Applicants with little or no experience making decisions should still be able to tell you what they consider the important factors based on what they've learned from their managers/supervisors.

> **Consider this:** *Experience doesn't guarantee good results. Applicants with experience as managers may still give you answers that you consider unsatisfactory.*

What was an important decision you made at your former/present job? What was the most difficult decision you made at your former/present job?

What an applicant considers the most important decision may not automatically be the most difficult decision. An important decision may have involved money at risk for the company, yet been a decision that the applicant felt comfortable making. The most difficult decision may have involved terminating a trusted, long-term employee. As important as the examples given by applicants is the manner in which they made the decisions.

> **Consider this:** *Watch for weakness portrayed as compassion, or bravado portrayed as confidence.*

How do you handle situations with difficult co-workers?

Some applicants will respond that they haven't had experience with difficult co-workers. This response may indicate a high level of tolerance or a high degree of skill in dealing with problem employees. They may, however, simply have been fortunate enough to work in pleasant situations. Question further to determine which is the case. For applicants who've encountered difficult co-workers, be especially aware of whether the difficulty was of a business nature or a personal nature (personality conflict, jealously or insensitivity).

Consider this: For applicants who admit to working with difficult employees, look for answers that show a positive attitude toward resolving the problem. What have they done to improve a negative situation?

Give me an example of a time when you had a disagreement with your supervisor.

Some applicants may state they never disagreed with their supervisor. If this is the case, listen to the tone of voice and manner in which they reply to decide whether you need to ask additional questions.

For applicants who admit to encountering such a situation, look for a positive approach to handling it. In addition, look for a good attitude concerning the resolution of the problem.

Consider this: Disagreements between a supervisor and someone he or she supervises is not uncommon. Most important is how the two parties resolved the situation and whether the applicant reveals angry feelings over past disagreements.

What type of employee do you find the most difficult to manage?

As with many other questions, the response to this one can tell you a lot about the applicant's personality and management skills. A workaholic may have difficulty managing people who are quite content to do the minimum and go home. Someone with an age bias may identify "older" or "younger" employees as a problem to manage. A manager who worked his or her way to the top may resent college graduates who enter at a high level within the company.

Some applicants will state they don't have difficulty managing any type of employee. Probe with additional questions to determine the accuracy of this statement.

> **Consider this:** *Someone who recognizes and acknowledges a shortcoming in managing people may be as valuable as the person who cannot or will not do so.*

THREE SPECIAL JOB TYPES: SALES, MANAGEMENT, AND TEMPORARY/PART-TIME POSITIONS

Jobs have pros and cons. What do you see as the pros and cons of selling?

The desired response should have more pros than cons, yet not ignore the cons. Look for answers that acknowledge the cons and reflect attitudes that can overcome them. An experienced and successful applicant who enjoys the field of sales will likely spend more time telling you about the good points of the job than the bad ones.

Consider this: Applicants new to the field of sales who have prepared for the interview may present you with some excellent answers. Ask additional questions to see if they truly understand their own answers.

Why do you consider yourself a successful salesperson? Or, Why do you believe you would be successful as a salesperson?

Success in the sales field usually requires someone with a high degree of self-confidence, the ability to handle rejection well, thorough product or service knowledge and the desire to work with customers. Applicants with experience in sales will likely answer with two or more of these qualities.

For applicants with no sales experience, you may need to question further to determine whether they have a chance at success as sales people. Previous employment, even though not in sales, may have given them experience in handling rejection, and working with customers.

Consider this: Every salesperson started as a novice at some point in time. Can you spot potential to become a super salesperson? Are you willing to hire someone who has potential?

Rejection is part of selling. How do you handle this aspect of the job?

Experienced and successful sales people know that rejection of the product or service isn't a rejection of them as individuals. Look for answers that show an ability to accept one customer's rejection and move on to the next. Answers should also indicate that the salesperson understands the need to try again, that a rejection today doesn't automatically mean a rejection on the next sales call.

> **Consider this:** *Applicants who seem uncertain about handling rejection, or appear distressed at the prospect, may be a poor choice even if they're strong in other areas.*

Why do you feel you're successful at cold calling?

Most sales positions involve some degree of cold calling; it's often the most distasteful part of the job. Successful sales people find ways to overcome their dislike. Use this question to find out which applicants successfully handle cold calling.

> **Consider this:** *Successful sales people often enjoy the challenge to their skills cold calling presents. People, who are afraid to approach people they don't know either by telephone or in person, may not be a good fit for your business and the work you have in mind.*

How satisfied have you been with past hiring decisions?

Even if applicants profess satisfaction with their hiring decisions, thoroughly check the "why" portion of the question. Good hiring decisions result in long-term, productive employees. If you discover a succession of short-term employees hired by an applicant, this may indicate he or she lacks interview skills, is difficult to work with, or simply makes poor hiring decisions.

> **Consider this:** *If the applicant admits to being less than satisfied with previous hiring decisions, try to find out why and what the person learned from previous hiring mistakes.*

How do you tell employees that you're not satisfied with their work?

An applicant's answer can reveal whether he or she handles such situations by ignoring them, over-reacting to them, or working for the common good of the employee, the department and the company. Another point to consider is whether the applicant indicates a desire to help employees reach a satisfactory level of performance or thinks the best solution is to terminate an employee and hire someone else.

> **Consider this:** *Effective managers deal with problems without undue delay, try to uncover the reason for the inadequate work, and*

then attempt to motivate and guide employees to higher levels of performance.

How do you encourage people to do their best?

Look for applicants that tell you about their personal methods for motivating employees, not just the company's system of evaluations and merit increases. Verbal and/or written compliments, immediate recognition of extra efforts, and unexpected small rewards from time to time can all help to motivate a workforce.

> **Consider this:** *A manager with the attitude that employees don't deserve recognition because they're paid to do the job does little to inspire loyalty.*

How do you offer constructive feedback?

No one enjoys criticism. For managers, however, giving constructive feedback is part of the job. The focus here is to learn how applicants give feedback to those that work for them. Applicants who seem willing to embarrass or put down employees may do little to help their employees improve their job performance.

> **Consider this:** *Managers who demean employees and then wonder why the situation doesn't improve don't understand the role or goal of constructive feedback.*

How do you prepare for performance appraisals?

Managers who use performance appraisals as growth tools for their employees know such appraisals consist of more than handing the employee a sheet of paper to "read and sign." They follow a method of objective goal setting rather than rating the employee on subjective and often non-job-related criteria.

> **Consider this:** *Look for responses of maturity and sensitivity when it comes to evaluating employee performance.*

What do you want your staff to do when they encounter problems?

Responses to this question should give a good indication of management style. Three managers may use somewhat different management styles, yet each in their own way be successful. Consider whether the applicant's answer reflects a style that will work within your company's culture.

> **Consider this:** *Some applicants may try to tell you what they think you want to hear instead of the way they actually approach such situations. If they don't sound comfortable or confident with their replies, ask for more information.*

What do you think might potentially interfere with your ability to work part-time?

Advise applicants early in the interview concerning what constitutes the part-time schedule, whether it will be a set or flexible number of hours each week, whether the schedule remains the same each week or will fluctuate. Then ask if this presents any difficulties. If the applicant hesitates, or makes qualifying remarks, such as, "Well, no, except for maybe on Tuesdays...," he or she may have reservations about the schedule but be reluctant to admit it.

> **Consider this:** *Applicants who are unenthusiastic about the schedule at the time of the interview may become even more unenthusiastic after they're employed.*

EXPLORING THE APPLICANT'S FUTURE PLANS

Tell me about your long-term employment goals.

Although it's not uncommon today for employees to move from one job to another, understanding an applicant's long-term goals may help you decide whether he or she is a good choice for employment. You may not want to invest time and money training someone whose long-term goal is to work in another field. If an applicant's long-term goal is to find an upper management job, and you know the position you want to fill offers no possibility for advancement, the likelihood is good that the individual will become a turnover statistic.

> **Consider this:** *An individual who has no long-term goals at the moment may possibly prove a better candidate for hire than someone with long-term goals that are incompatible with the job.*

Based on your understanding of this job, what aspects do you think you would find most satisfying?

This may initially seem an unlikely question to explore an applicant's future plans. However, the response can reveal more than the applicants intend. People interested in the job as a long-term position should be able to identify what they think they would find satisfying about the work. Those who intend to use the job only until they find something else may not have thought enough about this to provide a satisfactory answer.

> **Consider this:** *If at the time of the interview an applicant doesn't seem concerned about job satisfaction, it may be because he or she secretly doesn't plan to make a long-term commitment to your company.*

Where would you like to be in your job or career a year from now?

This question gives applicants an opportunity to prove they have given careful thought to their future, have at least some idea of how they plan to attain certain goals, and, hopefully, see your company as part of that future. This also allows them the opportunity to express desire for advancement and growth within the company.

> ***Consider this:*** *If where the applicant wants to be a year from now is incompatible with what he or she can attain within your organization, it's unlikely he or she will still be with you at the end of a year.*

What goals do you hope to achieve in your next job?

As in the previous question, the goals that applicants mention should be compatible with the position for which they're interviewing. Those who answer otherwise either don't understand the job for which they've applied or they're already, perhaps without realizing it, thinking past the next job.

> ***Consider this:*** *An applicant's goals for the "next job" should be ones that will also benefit the employer, not just the prospective employee.*

If you had a choice of any job and company, where would you go?

A great applicant may tell you, "This job and this company," and manage to convince you that he or she is sincere.

For the rest, whatever their responses, consider whether they talk about jobs and companies similar to the job for which they're interviewing or in a completely different field.

> **Consider this:** *A choice that has nothing in common with your industry or your company may be a signal that the interviewee already wishes he or she were somewhere else.*

WHAT QUESTIONS MIGHT THE APPLICANT ASK YOU?

At the end of the interview, most interviewers offer applicants an opportunity to ask questions. Sometimes these questions provide additional insight about the applicants as well as information that may not have come up during the interview. They can also provide the interviewer with an opportunity to clarify any misunderstandings about the job or the company.

What if the applicant doesn't ask any questions? It's possible that the interview was so exhaustive and thorough that you left no point uncovered. However, it's also possible that the applicant is so desperate for a job that he or she hesitates to ask anything for fear of asking the wrong question.

Another possibility is that the applicant failed to give complete attention to the interview and now hesitates to ask questions because he or she is unsure whether the interviewer may have already covered the subject.

The following questions represent thoughtful and legitimate inquiries for information by the applicant.

- What kind of training opportunities do you offer for possible advancement?

- How often would I have a performance evaluation and how long from hire date until the first evaluation?

- Is there a probationary period? If so, how long? Would I receive regular feedback on my performance during this period?

- What opportunity for growth does this position (or, the company) offer?

- Who does this position report to? How many people report to this position?

- What are the working hours for this position?

- Does the company have a dress code? Is this for everyone or only certain departments?

- What's the next step and when may I expect to hear from you?

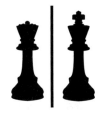

OTHER BOOKS
BY CAROL

***Retain or Retrain: How to Keep the Good Ones
from Leaving,*** **Co-author, InSync Press, 2001.**

Seven experts from varying experiential backgrounds have
pulled together to write this book of answers to the ever-
growing problem of employee turnover. How can a company regardless of its size keep good people from leaving for
greener pastures? This book offers practical solutions for
preventing your employees from slipping through your fin-
gers. It provides a variety of approaches to help managers
keep their talent base, even in a tight job market.

***366 Surefire Ways to Let Your Employees Know
They Count,*** **InSync Press, 2000.**

Sometimes employees need a little extra incentive to
encourage them to stick with you. People who enjoy what
they do and who they work with become more valuable to

the organization. They're usually happier as well. It's important for managers and business owners to encourage employees to reach their potential. Compensation isn't the only motivator. This book contains dozens of incentive ideas—many of them are quite simple but are often overlooked.

450 Low-Cost/No-Cost Strategies for recognizing, rewarding & retaining good people, 1999.

This is a breakthrough book on a hot topic! It contains hundreds of low-cost/no-cost ideas for rewarding and recognizing good performance as well as building fun into your organization. Many of the suggestions have been used before; others are new but are currently being successfully implemented in organizations of all kinds throughout North America. You can apply the ideas in this book immediately and with confidence.

Job Hunting in the 21st Century—Exploding the Myths, Exploring the Realities, St. Lucie Press, 1999.

Misconceptions about the job-hunting process have sabotaged the attempts of many job seekers. This book is about how to maintain the competitive edge in a business climate where the jobless rate has slipped to an over 30 year low. It brings the reader up to date on the realities of understanding and mastering the job search process. It provides concepts that are easy to apply and presents the most current information on how to find a job in today's job market. It examines the most common job-hunting myths and offers solutions for avoiding the pitfalls associated with each.

The Costs of Bad Hiring Decisions & How to Avoid Them—2nd Edition, St. Lucie Press, 1998.

This book is loaded with practical, easy-to-read, and understand tips for making sound and defensible hiring decisions. Learn how to keep your employment decisions healthy and profitable. From deciding what you're looking for in a candidate, to extending a job offer, this book will prove to be your on-the-shelf consultant.

Hiring Top Performers—350 Great Interview Questions For People Who Need People, **Revised 1998.**

Ideal for businesses of all sizes, in all industries, this book offers 350 sample interview questions in eight categories to help you get the information needed to make good hiring decisions. It's written in clear language and offers practical guidance to hiring managers at all levels.

The High Cost of Low Morale ...and what to do about it, **St. Lucie Press, 1996.**

Morale is an elusive quality. It's a feeling that's created within every employee. When morale is high, it's worth its weight in gold. When morale is low, the cost is tremendous. This book contains dozens of interviews with top business leaders that reveal inside tips for keeping employees motivated to do their best. It offers time-tested advice for leaders that will help keep your team energized and on track.

THREE OF CAROL'S MOST POPULAR WORKSHOPS

HOW TO COMPETE IN THE WAR FOR TALENT

Tired of fighting for good people? Is your team's performance a casualty of high turnover? Learn how to eliminate hiring decisions that are costing your business thousands! The average price of a regrettable choice can easily be one-third or more of the annual salary. If you're sick of employees that shine in the interview but tarnish quickly once employed, this workshop is for you. Never again transfer, promote or hire without being sure you're making the right decision the first time. Your attendance at this workshop will allow you to learn first-hand how to:

- Develop a broad-based sourcing strategy that balances the time it takes to hire with cost-per-hire.

- Insure a quality pool of top-notch candidates from which to choose.

- Recruit the right people, with the right skills, for the right jobs.

- Determine if candidates can do what they claim they can do.

- Decide what to ask and not ask to stay out of legal hot water.

- Get references to speak candidly, even in a litigation-happy society.

HOW TO BUILD A RETENTION CULTURE

This workshop offers state-of-the-art strategies for keeping your talent base, even in a tight job market. Low unemployment combined with increasingly aggressive recruiting has made retaining good people more and more difficult. Successful businesses have a strategic competitive advantage when reducing turnover; it's the key to satisfied and loyal customers. If you're looking for innovative, straightforward methodologies for retaining top talent, this workshop is a must-attend!

Part of what you will learn is how to:

- Analyze the marketplace to find out why you're losing good people to the competition.

- Use new-hire orientation to reinforce your business as the employer of choice.

- Align and develop the next generation of leaders with the company's strategic plan and objectives.

- Give critical feedback and still build employee loyalty, increase productivity and boost profits.

- Use exit interview data to help identify major contributing factors to turnover.

HOW TO TAKE THE GUESSWORK OUT OF INTERVIEWING

You become a valuable contributor to the corporate balance sheet by screening, interviewing and hiring quality people the first time. Mistakes go beyond losing the services of one person. There are administrative expenses and indirect costs to the business, including diminished productivity in the weeks before the employee leaves.

The ability to interview effectively has become a key recruitment tool. In this workshop you'll learn how to recruit for retention, not just fill a void on the organizational chart. Highlights of this presentation include:

- Innovative strategies for finding good people to interview.

- Learning to think like a marketer in promoting the benefits of working for you.

- Finding out how to determine the candidates' weaknesses.

- Incorporating structured, behavior-based interviewing techniques.

- The number one mistake interviewers make and how to avoid it.

- Using teams to recruit, interview and select top talent.

- Getting references to open up, even in a litigation-happy society.

ADDITIONAL READING

Arthur, Diane. *Recruiting, Interviewing, Selecting and Orienting New Employees.* New York, NY: AMACOM, 2000.

Axelrod, Alan. *Elizabeth I CEO: Strategic Lessons from the Leader Who Built an Empire.* Paramus, N.J: Prentice Hall Press, 2000.

Baum, David. *Lightening in a Bottle: Proven Lessons for Leading Change.* Chicago, IL: Dearborn, a Kaplan Professional Company, 2000.

Benton, D.A. *Secrets of a CEO Coach: Your Personal Training Guide to Thinking Like a Leader and Acting Like a CEO.* New York, NY: McGraw Hill, 1999.

Blanchard, Ken. *The Heart of a Leader: Insights on the Art of Influence.* Tulsa, OK: Honor Books, 1999.

Bradford, David L. with Allan R. Cohen. *Power Up: Transforming Organizations Through Shared Leadership.* New York, NY: John Wiley & Sons, 1998.

Buckingham, Marcus and Curt Coffman. *First Break All the Rules: What the World's Greatest Managers Do Differently.* New York, NY: Simon & Schuster Trade, 1999.

Deems, Richard S., Ph.D. *Hiring: How to Find and Keep the Best People.* Franklin Lakes, NJ: Career Press, 1999.

Drucker, Peter F. *Management Challenges for the 21st Century.* New York, NY: Harper Business, 1999.

Fein, Richard. *101 Hiring Mistakes Employers Make and How to Avoid Them.* Manassas Park, VA. Impact Publications, 2000.

Fry, Ron. *Ask the Right Questions, Hire the Best People.* Franklin Lakes, NJ: Career Press, 2000.

Green, Thad B. *Motivation Management: Fueling Performance by Discovering What People Believe About Themselves and Their Organization.* Palo Alto, CA: Davies-Black Publishing Limited, 2000.

Haasnott, Richard. *The New Wisdom of Business: 9 Guiding Principles From Today's Leaders.* Chicago, IL: Dearborn, a Kaplan Professional Company, 2000.

Hacker, Carol A. *Hiring Top Performers: 350 Great Interview Questions For People Who Need People.* Alpharetta, GA: 1998 revised.

Hacker, Carol A. *The Costs of Bad Hiring Decisions & How to Avoid Them 2nd Edition.* Boca Raton, FL: St. Lucie Press, 1999.

Hacker, Carol A. *450 Low-Cost/No-Cost Strategies for recognizing, rewarding & retaining good people.* Alpharetta, GA: 1999.

Hacker, Carol A. *366 Surefire Ways to Let Your Employees Know They Count.* Sanford, FL: InSync Press, 2000.

Harrell, Keith, *Attitude is Everything: 10 Life-Changing Steps to Turning Attitude into Actions.* New York, NY: Harper Collins Publishers, 2000.

Harris, Jim and Joan Brannick. *Finding and Keeping Great Employees.* New York, NY: AMACOM, 1999.

Harrison, Lawrence E. and Samuel P. Huntington. *Culture Matters: How Values Shape Human Resources.* New York, NY: Double Day, 2000.

Holton, Cher, Ph.D. *Living at the Speed of Life.* Raleigh, NC: Liberty Publishing Group, 1999.

Horowitz, Alan S. *The Unofficial Guide to Hiring and Firing People.* New York, NY: Macmillan USA, 2000.

Isler, Peter and Peter Economy. *At the Helm: Business Lessons for Navigating Rough Waters.* New York, NY: Double Day, 2000.

Kaye, Beverly and Sharon Jordan-Evans. *Love'EM or Lose'EM: Getting Good People to Stay.* San Francisco, CA: Berrett-Koehler Publishers, Inc., 1999.

Klinvex, Kevin C., Matthew S. O'Connell and Christopher P. Klinvex. *Hiring Great People.* New York, NY: McGraw Hill Companies, 1998.

Komisarjevsky, Chris and Reina. *Peanut Butter and Jelly Management,* New York, NY: AMACOM, 2000.

Krause, Donald G. *The Book of Five Rings for Executives.* London, England: Nicholas Brealey Publishing, 1999.

MacKoff, Barbara and Gary Wenet. *The Inner Work of Leaders.* New York, NY: AMACOM, 2000.

McCarter, John Lewis and Ray Schreyer. *Recruit and Retain the Best: Key Solutions for HR Professionals.* Manassas, VA: Impact Publications, 2000.

O'Malley, Michael N. *Creating Commitment: How to Attract and Retain Talented Employees by Building Relationships That Last.* New York, NY: John Wiley & Sons, 2000.

Rosenberg, Deanne. *A Manager's Guide to Hiring the Best Person for Every Job.* New York, NY: John Wiley & Sons, 2000.

Sanders, Don A. Ph.D., Carol A. Hacker, Lewis E. Losoncy, Ed.D., Ed Rose, Terry Yanovitch, David Cox, Ph.D., and David Baker, Ph.D. *Retain or Retrain: How to Keep the Good Ones From Leaving,* Sanford, FL: InSync Press, 2001.

Smart, Bradford D. *Topgrading: How Leading Companies Win by Hiring, Coaching and Keeping the Best People.* New York, NY: Prentice Hall, 1999.

Stettner, Morey. *Skills for New Managers,* New York, NY: McGraw-Hill, 2000.

Stevenson, Nancy. *Motivating People.* Indianapolis, IN: Macmillan USA, 2000.

Straub, Joseph T. *The Rookie Manager: A Guide to Surviving Your First Year in Management.* New York, NY: AMACOM, 2000.

Tulgan, Bruce. *Managing Generation X: How to Bring Out the Best in Young Talent.* New York, NY: Norton & Company, 2000.

INDEX

W

If you found this book thought provoking...
If you are interested in having this author...
or other of our consulting authors
design a workshop or seminar for your
company, organization, school, or team...

Let the experienced and knowledge group of experts at **The Diogenes Consortium** go to work for you. With literally hundreds of years of combined experience in:

Human Resources • Employee Retention
Management • Pro-Active Leadership • Teams
Encouragement • Empowerment • Motivation
Energizing • Delegating Responsibility
Spirituality in the Workplace
Presentations to start-ups and Fortune 100 companies,
tax-exempt organizations and schools
(public & private, elementary through university)

Call today for a list of our
authors/speakers/presenters/consultants
Call toll free at 866-602-1476
Or write to us at:
2445 River Tree Circle
Sanford, FL 32771